Learning Library

Classroom Management

Learning Books
Springhouse Corporation
Springhouse, Pennsylvania

Learning Library

vii, 183p. : ill.

SPRINGHOUSE CORPORATION BOOK DIVISION

Chairman
Eugene W. Jackson

Vice-Chairman
Daniel L. Cheney

President
Warren R. Erhardt

Vice-President, Book Operations
Thomas A. Temple

Vice-President, Production and Purchasing
Bacil Guiley

Program Director, Reference Books
Stanley E. Loeb

CLASSROOM MANAGEMENT

Editorial Director
Helen Klusek Hamilton

Art Director
John Hubbard

STAFF FOR THIS VOLUME

Editorial Services Manager: David R. Moreau

Copy Editors: Diane M. Labus, Doris Weinstock, Debra Young

Production Coordinator: Susan Hopkins Rodzewich

Designers: James J. Flanagan, Julie Carleton Barlow

Art Production Manager: Robert Perry III

Typography Manager: David C. Kosten

Typographers: Elizabeth A. DiCicco, Diane Paluba, Nancy Wirs

Senior Production Manager: Deborah C. Meiris

Assistant Production Managers: Pat Dorshaw, T.A. Landis

Indexer: Barbara Hodgson

Researcher: Nancy Lange

Editorial Assistants: Maree E. DeRosa, Denine Lichtfuss

Cover and Chapter Dividers
Illustrated by Ross Culbert
Holland & Lavery, NYC

Library of Congress Cataloging-in-Publication Data
Classroom management.
　(Learning library)
　Includes index.
　1. Classroom management.　　I. Series.
LB3013.C527　1987　　372.11'02　　87-10055
ISBN 0-87434-120-5

Contents

CONTRIBUTORS AND CONSULTANTS

EDITORIAL ADVISORY BOARD

Foreword

In a recent national survey, the Metropolitan Life Poll of American Teachers reported that one out of every four American teachers is dissatisfied with the profession and plans to leave it. One in three of these teachers cites lack of student motivation and discipline as a major reason for this dissatisfaction. Teachers want to see students who are better motivated; they want to spend less time on discipline; and they want to organize their classrooms in ways that promote students' achievements and self-worth.

Experienced teachers have learned to manage their classrooms well enough to cover most of the material they have planned—but there are additional techniques that can make their classroom experiences more rewarding for the teachers as well as for the students. In a collaborative effort, a number of experienced teachers have contributed their best classroom management strategies to a collective work, *Classroom Management,* the first volume in the LEARNING LIBRARY, a new series of books for teachers. This book provides practical suggestions that have worked well in real classrooms. These suggestions are designed to foster positive learning in students and satisfaction in teachers.

Classroom Management offers teachers practical suggestions based on actual classroom experience. In every chapter, the reader will find teacher-tested and approved methods for easier and more efficient management of day-to-day classroom problems. This volume covers everything from managing clutter to controlling the disruptive student. The opening chapter, Start the School Year Right, offers practical suggestions for planning and organizing in preparation for the new school year, including make-ahead projects. The next chapter, Help Students Get Acquainted, offers practical ways to ease students' adjustment to school, helping them get to know each other and quickly overcome new kid–new school–new teacher anxieties. Chapter 3, Get Going with Cooperation, offers strategies for helping students to work together through various games and specific methods of grouping in the classroom. Chapter 4, Cope with Recess, Restlessness, and Rainy Days, provides new things to do when the classroom seems too confining and even recess becomes stale and repetitive. Chapter 5, Improving the Classroom Environment, tells of some creative ways to arrange, decorate, and organize the classroom space into a pleasant place for learning. Chapter 6, Maintaining Discipline, offers classroom-tested methods that improve students' classroom behavior by helping them learn responsibility and self-discipline. Chapter 7, Making the Most of Special Activities, the final chapter, offers guidelines for foolproof planning and organizing techniques for special events and activities that put some sparkle into the daily classroom routine.

Throughout these chapters, various illustrations are used, as appropriate, to explain or enhance the text.

This volume, written by teachers for teachers, applies theory to classroom reality. Every elementary level teacher can find something useful in this book.

Maryanne Driscoll, PhD
Educational Consultant and
Coauthor of *The Successful Classroom*

1
START THE SCHOOL YEAR RIGHT

The old adage that says "Well begun is half done" surely applies perfectly to the school year. For good or ill, what happens in your classroom in the first few days sets the stage for the rest of the year. Your students' experiences in these first days of the school year can color the rest of the year with positive, enthusiastic attitudes that ease and enrich learning, or set up negative expectations of confusion, anxiety, or boredom.

Taking the time before school begins to plan classroom rules, organization, and activities will take your students smoothly through the first few days. More importantly, it will help you to enjoy a smoothly running classroom for the rest of the year. Read on for a collection of plan-ahead and start-up ideas that experienced teachers have found useful.

Summer: A time to organize and plan ahead

For everything there is a season, and certainly summer is the season for organizing, planning, and preparing for the upcoming school year—for reaffirming that commendable but elusive goal of "getting it together." And although summers are never long enough, you may find that there's still some time for school-related thoughts (as well as energy and motivation to follow up on them). Pondering new ideas for a new class and pulling things together—without the distraction of pressing school duties—can be enjoyable and may even inspire a renewed fondness for fall.

Getting out from under

The relationship between clutter and creativity is a matter of continuing debate, but most of us would risk being considered uncreative to be able to lay hands on that math game or art idea when it's needed. Yet clutter, creative or otherwise, seems to accumulate despite our best resolves. Is "getting out from under" an impossible task?

Organization can start with a thorough job of putting in order those teaching-idea clippings you've tucked away in fat file folders and bulging manila envelopes. It's well worth the time it takes.

A loose-leaf binder, the 6½-by-9-inch size, will accommodate clippings that are two columns wide, along with marginal notes. And for the ultimate in efficiency and smug satisfaction, prepare a notebook in a different color for each curriculum area. To complete your cataloging equipment, you'll need dividers with index tabs, tape, and plenty of filler paper.

The next step in your organizing endeavor is to read through the clippings—with one eye toward classification and the other toward quality. Sort clippings into major subject areas, making separate stacks for "definitely yes" items and "maybes." During this initial sorting you may become aware of subcategories within the major subject areas; make note of them but don't start new stacks at this point.

You're now ready to start taping the clippings onto the notebook sheets. Tape only one idea to a page. In this way you can shuffle ideas within categories or even transfer pages from one notebook to another.

✓ **Think small**

If your school has considered setting up a program of minicourses in special-interest areas, summer would be a good time to do some groundwork. A modified minicourse program lets students pursue such interests as cooking, small-engine repair, dramatics, chorus, square dancing, needlework, ceramics, languages, and much more, meeting once a week under the guidance of school staff and community resource persons. Tips on summer planning include both positive suggestions and cautionary notes on the mechanics of setting up.

From the outset, keep costs in mind; some kinds of crafts materials can be very expensive. But money needn't be a barrier: Look for a parent group to help with funding. Checking this possibility out well in advance of final

Reserve a large area (the living room floor, for example) for a final classification of ideas. Prepare a large label sheet for each subcategory you decide to use. Lay out the label sheets and sort the notebook pages onto them. When you're satisfied that each clipping is where it belongs, reassemble subject areas and insert each collection into its notebook. Finish up by preparing category tabs. If you still have some "maybe" items lying around, include them with the established categories, make new categories, or toss them out (you *can* do it!).

You might also prepare envelopes or folders (color-coded to match the subject-sorted idea inventories you've made) to receive the clippings that you'll be stacking up during the coming year. For the moment, however, you're caught up and ready to put your uncluttered collection to creative use.

planning will help you set your sights on realistic goals.

During the summer, also check out craft fairs, art-in-the-park shows, flea markets, library and university lectures, service club bazaars and benefits, and locally produced TV and radio programs to track down artisans, collectors, and experts in various fields who might be interested in teaching a minicourse.

Meanwhile, draft a questionnaire through which students can indicate the kinds of things they'd like to learn about—crafts they'd like to try, skills they'd like to master. Although the activities ultimately offered will depend upon the reservoir of skilled leaders you're able to secure, students' interests will be a prime consideration. (Special efforts may need to be made later on to find instructors in unexpectedly popular areas of interest.)

Think through the logistics of the pro-gram—the hour that might work best as a regular activity time slot, the sizes of groups that may be accommodated by various activities (perhaps as many as 32 in a square-dancing group, 10 or fewer in a group requiring closer supervision), and procedures for making group assignments in an equitable manner. Discuss expectations and responsibilities at the outset and develop contingency plans. Although the specifics of your activity-time program may not be finalized until fall, now is an ideal time for planning, researching, and seeking minicourse leaders.

ELEVEN PRESCRIPTIONS FOR EFFECTIVE CLASSROOM MANAGEMENT

In recent studies to evaluate good learning environments, educators identified 11 prescriptions for effective classroom management.

1. Ready the Classroom
Be certain your classroom space and materials are ready for the beginning of the school year.

2. Plan Rules and Procedures
Decide before the year begins what behaviors are acceptable or unacceptable in your classroom. Then think about what procedures students must follow to participate in class activities, to learn, and to function effectively in a school environment.

3. Plan Consequences
Decide ahead of time what consequences will follow appropriate and inappropriate behavior in your classroom, and communicate these rules to your students. Then be sure to follow these rules consistently.

4. Teach Rules and Procedures
In your lesson plan, include how, when, and in what sequence you will teach rules or procedures on each day and when relearning or practice will occur.

5. Select Beginning School Activities Carefully
Develop activities for the first few days of school that readily involve the students and maintain a whole-group focus.

6. Plan Strategies for Potential Problems
Plan strategies to deal with the potential problems that could upset your classroom organization and management. Be especially aware of problems that could interfere with your monitoring or could teach students bad habits.

7. Monitor Student Behavior Closely
Look for students who don't follow procedures or who don't finish or even start assignments; violations of rules or other uncooperative or deviant behavior; and appropriate behavior.

8. Stop Inappropriate Behavior
Intervene promptly to stop inappropriate and disruptive behavior: it won't go away by itself.

9. Organize Instruction
Organize instruction to provide learning activities at suitable levels for all students in your class.

10. Make Students Accountable
Develop procedures that keep your students responsible for their own work.

11. Present Clear Instruction
Be clear when you present information and give directions to your students.

Make-ahead projects

Vacation time also offers an opportunity for you to assess your repertoire of fantastic feats and dazzling devices, and to consider adding some new material. Here are learning aids that you can put together in summer for the next fall season.

Social Studies

EARLY GRADES

Moving in the right direction

For reinforcing cardinal directions, games are great. These two can be put together easily before the first day of school.

• **Travel the States.** Use a wall map of the U.S. as a game board to build children's familiarity with directions as well as with the 48 continental states. Children "travel" the country via toy car, cardboard airplane, miniature bird, or even broomstick, following the dictates of two spinners.

Each spinner shows a circle marked into quadrants. On one circle are the numerals 1 through 4; on the other are the four cardinal directions. Indicator arrows are secured in place with paper fasteners.

Students place their "vehicles" in a starting state—their home state, a state you're studying, or one determined by some other means. The first player spins to find in which direction he or she will travel. (The direction spun may mean that the player is stuck in the state for that turn; there's simply nowhere east of Flor-

ida to go.) If a move is possible, the player spins to find the number of spaces (i.e., states) he or she can move in this turn. The aim is to travel through as many states as possible within a predetermined time limit. Each player/traveler keeps a running list (giving always-good-to-have practice in writing state names correctly).

• **Design directions.** Try a game in which students follow "direction directions" to make designs on graph paper. The single make-ahead game element is a spinner/compass that includes intermediate directions. (If you prepare the compass as an overhead transparency, the whole class can play at once.)

Each player is provided with graph paper. The first move is to mark point A in the center of the paper. The next move is dictated by a spin of the compass arrow. Starting at point A, players count five spaces in the direction indicated to locate point B. The arrow is spun again and, starting from point B, each player counts five spaces in the new direction to locate point C. After plotting and labeling five points, players draw connecting lines in alphabetical sequence, ending up at point A. (A glance at the resulting pattern should reveal direction-following prowess.)

MIDDLE GRADES

Perpetual time line

Create and maintain a time line to put historical events in perspective and to encourage students to do research for items to add.

You might construct the bare bones of the time line in summer by marking a roll of paper into segments for 10-year intervals. But space in the classroom is going to be an important consideration; you'll need to decide on a loca-

tion where the time line can be accessible throughout the year.

Insert a few major events to begin the time-lining process. But don't fill in too much: the more open space that stares out at the students the better, for these are spots that their research can fill.

Student additions to the time line should be written (or illustrated) on index cards, posted above or below the line, and connected to it with yarn. Older students should identify the sources of their information. Entries can be labeled with the researchers' names, too, if that seems appropriate.

As an ever-developing element of the classroom environment, the time line can serve as a discussion starter and research-report stimulator, as well as a reminder of the continuous nature of history.

Language Arts

EARLY GRADES

Pictures worthy of words

You never can have too many pictures, as most teachers know. While you conscientiously (even compulsively) cut pictures from magazines this summer, keep in mind these two language arts activities.

- **Captions for sentence building.** Use pictures to give young children practice in making up complete sentences. Look for and clip out pictures of stimulating, story-evoking scenes. Mount each picture at the top of a large piece of construction paper.

In the classroom, gather the children to study and discuss the content of the various pictures. Convert several responses raised by your what-do-you-see queries into examples of complete sentence captions, and write them below the appropriate scenes. Then open the floor to children's sentence contributions.

Suggest that children search at home (or in magazines that you provide) for pictures they'd like to caption. Set aside a display area to showcase the scenes and prepare strips of paper to use for dictated sentence captions. Label sentences with contributors' names. After caption writers have had ample opportunity to concentrate on simple declarative sentences, have them try captions in the form of questions (or convert a few of the statements to questions). The scenes-and-sentences gallery should become quite a conversation place.

- **Put yourself in the picture.** Try a direct-action approach to pictures as a way of stimulating language. Be on the alert for large pictures of appealing environments, rich in

detail—home interiors, street scenes, natural settings. Present the pictures as places children might walk into and explore, or places where they might observe friends or family.

Invite each child to select a picture as his or her private domain. Provide markers, modeling clay and other art materials for children to use to add elements to the scenes—people, animals, objects. Pictures thus personalized provide the child with an insider's view of the environment—the better to write lively, imaginative narratives with an "I-was-there" element of realism.

MIDDLE GRADES

Unlisted spelling list

Here's an idea for bringing new life to the spelling list.

Review last year's basic spelling words, recalling areas of difficulty as well as successful approaches to various word peculiarities. Make a card for each word. On one side of the card write the word's phonetic spelling; on the other side write the word and bracket the syllables. Red flag those words that are rule breakers (or use red cards for these words). Color code other categories—for example, words with affixes, words beginning with diagraphs, words with silent letters.

Regroup the color-coded cards into weekly lesson sets, make appropriate dividers to identify and separate the sets, and store the cards in a shoe box.

The spelling cards can then be used for one-to-one spelling practice or for games with small groups. Children may also test themselves by trying to spell from the phonetic side. You may find that the spelling box itself seems to acquire the status of a game—a welcome switch from the familiar "Oh no, spelling" response to the traditional list.

Science

EARLY GRADES

Adopt a tree

Whatever the size of your class for the upcoming year, you can consider taking on an additional chore. Give some thought to "adopting" a tree.

Start looking this summer for a likely candidate. Trees that lose their leaves, change colors, or have blossoms (maples, magnolias, fruit trees) provide more dramatic study opportunities than trees that undergo less obvious seasonal changes. If your schoolyard provides an inadequate selection, check out a nearby park or the neighborhood streets.

Plan for routine seasonal visits: a meet-our-tree orientation in early fall, a trip at the time of color change or leaf drop as the days grow shorter, a visit when the branches are bare, an excursion when leaf buds are opening in spring. On in-between visits, children may engage in more detailed investigations—noting the size and shape of the tree and its leaves; inspecting the bark and branching patterns; looking for signs of environmental interaction, such as the visits of living creatures and the effects of weather.

Discuss class findings and encourage follow-up research based on such questions as: What are the visible changes in the tree with the change of season, and what causes those changes? What changes in the tree are caused by living things, including humans? How do changes in the tree affect living and nonliving things?

Activities arising from a tree adoption might include: keeping a record book and illustrating it with photos and artwork; keeping an imaginative diary from the tree's point of view; researching the tree's family and related species; researching the tree's economic value and ecological role; writing poems describing observations and expressing feelings about the tree; writing stories in which the tree has a starring role; measuring the tree's circumference and calculating its height.

Welcome a tree as a class member and you'll be tapping a wealth of projects and activities through which class members learn about plant processes and the seasonal cycle.

MIDDLE GRADES

Dear Dr. Know-it-all

You may find that winding up a health unit can be a fun-for-all experience when Dr. Know-it-all can be persuaded to participate. You can

ensure the good doctor's involvement by making preparations this summer.

Dr. Know-it-all is patterned quite loosely after the gurus of medical advice columns. The doctor's role is undertaken by students completing the health unit, while you—by means of task card "letters"—take on the roles of an assortment of long-suffering patients with a wide variety of ills, all based on information covered in the unit. For example:

Dear Dr. Know-it-all,
Mean Mike Mott put a toad in my lunchbox two weeks ago, and now I have a wart on my hand. I blame Mike and his toad for my condition. How can I get rid of the wart?

—Toad-hating Tandra

The doctor's reply will exonerate the toad and explain theories about viruses and warts, and will advise that removal of the wart be left to a doctor. (On the matter of lunchbox viola-

tion, the doctor is free to prescribe whatever remedy seems fitting.)

Other letters might cite self-image concerns brought on by freckles, sunburn, or allergic rashes. You might find that having kids serve as professionals by proxy can have a healthy effect on the classroom climate.

Mathematics

EARLY GRADES

No-trouble doubles

Try this math aid that can help young children to focus on the "doubles" addition facts, $1 + 1$ through $9 + 9$.

Look around this summer for ordinary everyday "doubles" items (or pictures of the items) that are likely to have child appeal. For starters, here are some sample doubles:

$1 + 1$: a pair of socks or mittens

$2 + 2$: wheels on a toy car; legs on a dog

$3 + 3$: a grasshopper's legs; eyelets in a shoe

$4 + 4$: an eight-pack soft drink carton; a spider's legs

$5 + 5$: fingers on two hands; toes on two feet

$6 + 6$: an egg carton

$7 + 7$: two-week section of a calendar (Pick a month that begins on Sunday and use the first two-week block to minimize confusion.)

$8 + 8$: a box of 16 crayons, 2 rows of 8 each

$9 + 9$: players on a baseball or volleyball team.

Display your doubles for the children to explore. Have them count items, compare sets and match quantities with doubles number sentences. Quite likely, some children will begin to search out additional doubles to display, perhaps doubling your original stock.

MIDDLE GRADES

Recycling receipts

If your summer turns out to be one when you hardly have any time to breathe, you may be interested in a math idea that doesn't require cutting, pasting, drawing, labeling, or laminating. This math project is simply a matter of collecting—specifically, sales slips and cash register receipts. You should be able to accumulate a considerable quantity and a fascinating variety within a few weeks.

Transforming these records of summertime transactions into math materials will be a responsibility for your new class to tackle: Provide each student with a collection of sales receipts. After examining the receipts, the student formulates ten questions, some involving computation, others calling for attention to specific details. Some examples:

Put all the receipts in order from the highest total to the lowest. Where was the most money spent? The least? What is the difference in totals?

At which store was the greatest number of items bought?

How much money was spent for produce at the supermarket on July 6?

How much more money was spent for groceries on August 10 than on August 22?

How much more tax was charged on shoes than on the fan belt?

What is the average price of items purchased at the stationery store?

If you paid only half the bill at the hardware store, how much would you owe?

The student then puts the questions and the set of receipts into an envelope, and exchanges envelopes with a classmate. If each student keeps an answer key for the questions ex-

changed, the two exchangers may compare and discuss their answers, adding a self-checking and correcting feature to the activity.

Reading

EARLY GRADES

Story boxes

You will delight the young children in your new class—while you provide excursions into literature—with the story boxes you create this summer.

Look for sturdy boxes with hinged lids. (Cigar boxes are ideal, as are some stationery

boxes and pencil boxes.) Cover the inside surface of each box lid with felt to make a miniature display board. Inside the box place storytelling figures and props cut from felt or another nonfraying fabric that will adhere to the display board.

You can use a story box to introduce a favorite tale. Reproduce and cut out figures from the book's illustrations and place them in the box. Then as you tell the story, position the various cutouts to portray each scene. Later children can take the box and retell the story or adapt it in imaginative ways. Story boxes can also be stocked with amazing characters and props to stimulate do-it-yourself stories.

If you teach older children, you might suggest they make story boxes as gifts for younger family members or a primary grade class.

The compact, portable, keep-the-pieces-together story boxes are perfect for children to use independently at odd moments. But their most fascinating feature is the way their contents can change and grow daily.

MIDDLE GRADES

Judging books by their titles

If you have summer access to the school library, you might start preparing an activity that helps students "discover" worthwhile books they might otherwise overlook.

Search out books that fall within the reading range of your class but that are not already familiar to your students. Look for intriguing, even somewhat puzzling, titles. Prepare a card for each title in this off-the-beaten-path book collection.

Introduce the activity to your class by discussing the functions of a book title, such as identifying the book and arousing interest by hinting at what's inside. Then give each student one of the title cards. Ask students to speculate about characters, setting, and plot, and to prepare brief written summaries of their ideas. Make clear that the point is to draw on imagination rather than to "guess right" about the relationship of the title to the story.

Following the writing of the summaries, students try to find out the actual significance of the titles. First stop: the card catalog. Does the annotation on the title card explain how the book might have earned its name? More than likely, students will need to go to the shelves for more information. And in skimming for the meaning behind the title, a researcher just might get hooked on the book.

The activity concludes with a general "what's in a title" discussion. But you might suggest that students withhold some of the details of their specific title/book findings: A little mystery may lure another reader.

RATE YOUR OWN MANAGEMENT STYLE: EFFECTIVE OR INEFFECTIVE?

When planning procedures for the new school year, review your own classroom behaviors. Compare your own patterns of classroom behavior to the lists below and evaluate your effectiveness as a classroom manager.

Effective Classroom Managers...

- plan the first day to provide maximum contact with and control of students.

- offer interesting activities.

- stay with the students throughout class time.

- clearly explain the classroom system, using examples and reasons.

- limit first instructions to *necessary* rules and procedures (use of the bathroom, pencil sharpener, and water fountain); avoid overloading students with procedural information.

- spend enough time reexplaining and reminding students about rules. Don't consider students fully prepared after a day or two.

- offer a variety of rewards and signals for appropriate behavior.

- give specific assignments while handling clerical tasks but continue to monitor.

- stop inappropriate behavior promptly.

- introduce content and additional procedures gradually and in an enjoyable way and don't rush into workbooks or readers.

Ineffective Classroom Managers...

- busy themselves with housekeeping or clerical duties during the first few critical days.

- allow students to wander around.

- leave the room often during the first few hours of the school year.

- often use vague rules, such as "Be in the right place at the right time."

- don't think through their rules and procedures.

- don't clearly explain their rules for using the bathroom, and so forth; give rules without rehearsing or reinforcing them.

- give little notice and reinforcement to students who obey the rules.

- fail to monitor the classroom closely.

- give frequent threats or warnings without follow through, causing students to push limits.

Start-up ideas with staying power

Whether you're a methodical long-distance planner or a last-minute scrambler, it's hard to feel completely "ready" for school to begin. As you're warming up, you might look over these suggestions for meeting the new year and those new learners.

A bulletin board with personality

Here's an idea that could help clothe your bare bulletin boards. The before-opening-day preparation for this project consists of backing the bulletin board, placing the word *ME* in the center and making a name card for each child on your class list. On the first day of school, adjust your name card collection to reflect last-minute additions and withdrawals and then post the names randomly around the *ME* on the bulletin board.

Challenge fresh-from-summer students to think of as many words as they can to describe people they know, themselves included. Suggest that they think carefully about how these people look and act. As children translate these images into descriptive words, list their contributions on the chalkboard. With vocabulary building in mind, you might initiate discussion to clarify meanings and to explore connotations of the words offered by the class.

The next step is for each child to choose a favorite word and to make a picture illustrating its meaning. (Suggest that each child have a second and third choice ready.) Establish a system through which children can register their choices and, as a word is chosen, circle the selection to show it has been taken. When the illustrations are finished and titled with their respective descriptors, have the children post their pictures on the *ME* bulletin board.

Now have the children focus their thoughts on themselves. Invite them to browse through the pictures while pondering, "Which words best describe me?" Each child chooses three words, and this time no one gets sole claim on a word; any number can choose the same one.

Provide the children with tacks and string they can use to connect their chosen words with their names. The *ME* bulletin board, replete with "personality strings," can become a discussion starter and get-acquainted center—as well as a room brightener.

High-flying calendar

Here's another room-brightening idea—for now and throughout the school year. It's a useful learning device and reference tool, and it doesn't take a bit of floor or wall space. It's a circular calendar—all 12 months in a continuous belt—that can be suspended from the

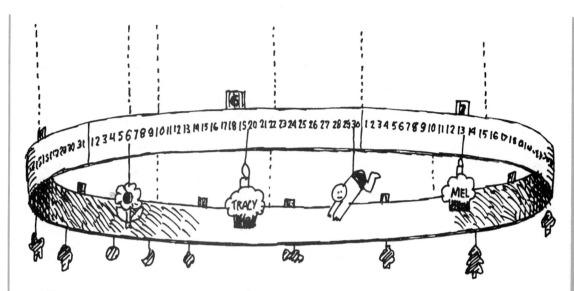

ceiling. Students can read around the year by circumnavigating the calendar's circumference.

Prepare 12 white posterboard strips that are about 6 inches wide and 40 inches long. Label each strip with the name of a month and leave a border space about an inch deep along the length of each strip, both top and bottom. Write the dates for the months in a continuous line. Color the top and bottom borders to indicate the seasons: orange for fall (September 23 to December 21), blue for winter (December 22 to March 19), green for spring (March 20 to June 20), yellow for summer (June 21 to September 21). At the top of each month's strip attach a number to show the position of that month in the year (e.g., September would be marked 9; October, 10). Laminate the posterboard for durability.

Staple the months together in a ring and punch holes at 30-inch intervals. Decide on the appropriate elevation for the calendar—out of the way but not so high that it's out of reading range. Attach one end of a length of

sturdy string or fishing line to each punched hole. On the other end of each string fasten a paper clip that has been opened up to make a hook. Suspend the calendar from the ceiling panel strips.

You might consider some accessories to further enhance your hanging calendar:

Birthday reminders in the form of tag board cupcakes can be inscribed with children's names, decorated and hung from the appropriate dates.

Day-of-the-week markers indicating the school days—"Today is Monday," etc.—can be prepared. Glue a snap clothespin on the back of each day's marker. Every morning the appropriate marker may be clipped in place. You might also make five "Tomorrow will be…" and "Yesterday was…" markers in the same style. These could be clipped on the calendar itself or clipped to the marker for the day.

Seasonal scenes, holiday pictures and red-letter-day reminders can be sprinkled throughout the year.

The hanging calendar is handy for young children who are learning the names of the days and the months. Children can be challenged to determine the number of days (or months, weeks, and days) until a birthday or other special event, to find which month has the most birthdays, or to discover which months have the most school days.

The calendar demonstrates the continuous cycle of months and keeps the total year in view (and in mind)—and it gives summer birthdays the recognition that they often miss.

Meet the senior class

Try this getting-to-know-us idea for those of you with a sixth grade class or other "oldest class in the school" group. These students are about to take on the distinction of being "seniors," a position in which they—quite unintentionally and oftentimes unwillingly—become role models for the younger children in the school.

One way of launching these seniors in a manner that can cultivate both a sense of pride and a sense of responsibility is a "Meet the Senior Class" day. Ask your incoming students to start gathering materials that will provide information about their interests, hobbies, milestone experiences, achievements, "favorites," etc., and to collect items such as photos, posters, sports gear, artwork, samples from collections, books, and favorite foods. Each student then prepares an exhibit that expresses his or her personality.

Arrange for display space—in the gym, cafeteria, or even outdoors—for the "Meet the Senior Class" exhibit. Each senior (perhaps wearing a favorite outfit, souvenir hat, message T-shirt) is the host at his or her display as the other children in the school, a class at a time, visit the senior class exposition.

As the younger visitors discover appealing items in the various displays, the interaction between the older and younger students comes quite naturally. Even somewhat shy seniors find it's not difficult to talk when they're discussing familiar topics on a one-to-one basis. Most students can feel confident that they have expertise of some sort to share.

A seniors' day can be a festive time for all. And who knows, you may be starting a tradition. Fifth graders may begin to store up ideas for their big moment next fall, when everyone gets to know *them*.

Dial a special day

Although everyone's first-day experiences and encounters can seem unforgettably vivid, chances are good that as routine sets in, you and the class will find one week blending into another, blurring images and impressions. Before this begins to happen, you might establish some ways of recording events and preserving

ideas so that the experiences of this year can become a more tangible memory for all.

You can try this memory preserving plan you can call "Dial-a-Day." During the first week of school the children prepare special booklets for recording their thoughts. The booklets are composed of round pages about 5 inches in diameter. The booklet cover resembles a telephone dial (no extra charge for fancy colors) with the school year months marked in the "holes." To carry the telephone theme further, children may trace a "dial" circle in the center of each booklet page. Ideally there would be a page for each day of the school year—perhaps organized by month or by quarter—but this may not be practical, and the booklets could easily serve for special, rather than daily, recording.

Pages are punched (stick-on reinforcements can cut down on "fallout") and tied together with colorful yarn. Then a Dial-a-Day booklet—ready for when-the-mood-strikes recording—is attached to each child's desk. The child writes the date in the center of a page—in the dial circle—and in the ring surrounding the dial, the child jots impressions: "Kim is back this year!" "The cafeteria is orange. Yuk." "Music is going to be my favorite subject."

Booklets can be private, or children may choose to share excerpts. As the booklets become filled, you might collect them and put them away until the end of the school year, when they can be returned as personal mementos—and fascinating reading matter.

Reporter of the week

To capture and keep the year's events and ideas with sound, designate a "reporter of the week"—just as you appoint students for other rotating classroom jobs—to make a tape recording summarizing classroom happenings for the week. The reporter must be attentive to the week's happenings in the ongoing program as well as to special events—humorous moments, times of excitement, shared sadness. Other students can assist the reporter by submitting story ideas throughout the week. In introducing the reporter-of-the-week idea, you might discuss the sorts of items that seem to be weekly report material. But assure the students that each reporter will have considerable freedom in choosing material.

Using notes or perhaps an outline, the reporter organizes collected material by categories or in chronological order. Writing a report could be an option—a challenge for some, an unreasonable chore for others. (This news gathering activity may lead to research about newspaper and broadcast reports and reporting, discussion of news stories, human

interest stories, commentary, and so forth.)

Reporting to the class is an every-Friday event, and students may want to devise a TV or radio "studio" setting where the action can take place. The reporter begins the tape by giving his or her name and identifying the week being reviewed. Some students may want to create individual "signature" phrases for signing off their reports.

Tapes are preserved as a weekly log of the year's events. They can be played back as an individual or group activity, both for enjoyment and for historical research.

Self-portraits for now and then

Consider this project that helps to close as well as to open the school year. It's called September Day.

The activity begins with children creating first-day-of-school self-portraits—full-length to show everyone from hairdo to footgear. You may want to post the pictures (if one of those bulletin boards is still empty), but then collect the portraits for your September Day file.

Also during the first week of school or early in the year, collect samples of each child's work in all subject areas. (Try to include such items as math fact checkups and other such milestones.) Store all of these materials in the September Day file to await the last week of school. Then you proclaim a September Day. On that day—after the usual morning routine—begin a reading instruction time with tasks patterned after those of that long-ago first week of school: easy vocabulary, simple stories from beginning-of-the-year-level readers and worksheets to match. You may even be able to reassemble the original reading groups. In all subject areas the theme is "remember September." All students get to take that first-level math facts test over again. They'll be amazed to discover that what took some children 12 minutes to complete is now polished off by everyone within 2 minutes, and most papers will be perfect. Everyone makes a new self-portrait too. Have the children collect their morning's work. (All the September Day's assignments can most likely be completed by noon.)

In the afternoon, pull out the September Day file and distribute the contents to the children. Let them browse through the work they did 9 months earlier. It's exciting to compare what they did at the start of the year—especially in handwriting and composition—with what they're able to accomplish in the spring.

Have the children organize their own materials into take-home booklets. The September self-portrait goes facedown on the desk with all September work facedown on top of the portrait. The work of the June day is placed faceup on the stack with the new self-portait resting on top. The double booklet makes a satisfying study in contrasts.

Note for schools with a large turnover between September and June. You might try collecting a "first day" assortment of papers whenever a new child comes and return a child's collection whenever a student leaves; that way children have an opportunity to do at least some short-term comparing. Without much fuss there can be something on file for each child to look over and to enjoy on September Day next June.

"The readiness is all," remarked Hamlet, pretty well summarizing the September situation. The observation both admonishes and exhorts as each teacher prepares to meet a bold new class. A stumbling start on the year can be a distinct handicap, for a driving pace will be set early. Readying yourself can involve making the room a welcoming place with a few special touches, planning activities that help students settle into their new situation successfully, and building among students a "historical" sensitivity, encouraging them to record ideas, events, and accomplishments as the new school year flashes by.

Welcome your students 18 unforgettable ways

The world, claims T.S. Eliot, will end with a whimper. But that's no reason your school year can't start with a bang.

Here's a collection of showstarters designed to get kids thinking and imagining from the first minute. Most of the ideas easily adapt to all grade levels, and generally they suggest follow-up activities that can take your class right into the basics and beyond.

Take "Meeting the staff" (6), in which the school secretary, the janitor, and other school workers visit your room to say hello and to explain their jobs. You could have your students conduct interviews. Asking questions, listening, and asking follow-up questions—perhaps with you modeling these behaviors—provide a solid language arts opener.

We hope the items presented here will help you create a mood of excitement that will nurture the learning experiences you have in store for your children this year.

1
Invite a keynoter
Invite a famous or outstanding local citizen (the mayor, a television personality) to deliver a back-to-school pep talk to your class. The message can be delivered live, on tape, or in the form of a letter.

2
Advertise
The day before the start of school, greet your students with a classified ad placed in the personal section of your local newspaper. Although your students may not read the ad, many of their parents will see it and read it to the children.

ATTENTION THIRD GRADE STUDENTS

To my third grade students at Walter Hays Elementary School: I'm looking forward to seeing you tomorrow.
—Your teacher, Ann Martin

Clip the advertisement and post it where students can see it when they arrive the first day.

If you would rather not advertise, send a letter with a similar mesage to all of your students.

3
Fearlessly forecast
Invite your class to recall some of the big events of last year. These could be things that happened in their class, in town, or nationally—who won the World Series, for example.

Now ask your students to join you in making predictions for the coming year. You might prime their imaginations with the following predictions:
• Scientists will learn how to control a person's moods from a distance by beaming mood messages directly to the brain.
• Smoking will be forbidden in public.
• Wearing seat belts will be legally required

in all states.

- Talking toys will be the rage.

You, the teacher, can make safe predictions about what the kids will learn: "By March 1988, you children will know how to solve a hard math problem like this! And by May, you will all know how to spell every word on this list."

Write the predictions on a "Futures Poster" that you can display in the room.

4

Don't just say "Hello"

Greeting your class for the first time can be a special moment. You can magnify it by welcoming the children in several different languages. Here are nine greetings used by teachers around the world. You might teach some or all of these expressions to your students, who can share the greetings with their families.

Mandarin Chinese:

進学おめでとう

(hwan nying ru sywe)
Welcome to enter your studies.

Hebrew:

ברוכים הבאים לבית הספר

(bru heem hoc hozreem lvayt hasayfar)
Blessed be the returners to school.

Spanish:

¡ BIENVENIDOS A LA ESCUELA!

(bee en benidoes ah la eskwala)
Welcome to the school.

French:

BIENVENUS À L'ÉCOLE

(byen vneu ah laycull)
Welcome to the school.

Japanese:

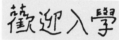

(shin gakoone o may day toe)
Congratulations on the new school year.

German:

SEID HERZLICH WILLKOMMEN IN DER SCHULE

(zide hairt-slick vilkomen in dur skoo-luh)
A hearty welcome to the school.

Russian:

ПРИВЕТСТВУЕМ ВАС В ШКОЛЕ

(privetstruyem vas f schkoyeh)
We welcome you in school.

Swahili:

KARIBUNI TENA SHULENI

(ca[r] eeboony tayna shulayni)
Welcome all of you to school.

Vietnamese:

CHAÒ MỪNG BAN TRỞ LAI TRƯỜNG

(nchow meung bong tchar lie tcherung)
Welcome, friends, back to school.

5

Get your bearings

Following Labor Day, school becomes an important focus in the lives of children. You might give them an unusual view of the school building itself by bringing in an aerial photograph of the school neighborhood. Aerial photographs are available from aerial photo companies (look in the yellow pages under "Photographers, aerial"), city halls, and some private real estate developers. You could point out that an important function of learning in general is to provide people with new perspectives on familiar things. What kinds of things can the children discover about their school by studying the aerial photograph?

Of course, students will enjoy trying to find familiar landmarks on the photograph. If you bring in a corresponding street map, you can build a nice beginning lesson on mapping. (What's on the photo that's not on the map? What's on the map that's not on the photo? When would the map be more handy? When the photo?)

The aerial photo-map experience might lead to a metaphorical discussion of the year's "journey": Where is the class now? Where is it going? You might talk about *learning landmarks* you expect to pass along the way.

6

Meeting the staff

Ask the principal, the school nurse, the librarian, the janitor, the school secretary, and any other important figures to deliver brief greetings and to explain their jobs to your class. They could drop by during the first day. Or, the day before school, you might record them on tape and then play the tape back for your class. A tape such as this can be loaned to other classes.

7

Share your summer

Tell what *you* did this past summer. If you took any home movies, here's a chance for you to show them to perhaps the most appreciative audience you'll ever find. Even if you don't have any home movies, share your summer experiences—especially any photos or postcards from faraway places.

8

Give a "pop" quiz

Here's an unusual alternative to the "what did you do this summer" routine. Give the quiz on page 26, which is about students' activities during summer vacation. Although this quiz is intended to be fun to take, it has a useful function. It not only gives you information about your students and their summer vacation experiences but also allows everyone to start the school year with a success. The test is designed so that every kid gets at least 100 points. It can be given orally to nonreaders, who can respond with a show of hands.

9

Recall the past

The beginning of every school year is a historic moment. You can put it into perspective for kids by helping them discover what it was like when their parents were in the same grade. One possibility is to obtain an old issue of the town newspaper from about 25 years ago. Show the pictures. Read stories that tell what was happening at home and elsewhere. What were the main concerns of the day? How do they compare with today's issues? What were the ads selling?

If your local newspaper publisher can't lend you an old issue, try the library. Many libraries keep past issues that you can copy. The pictures probably won't come out too well, but at least you can read the stories.

Another source for local history would be your town's historical society, which is often nested in the library.

For a more global look at the past, try borrowing old copies of *Life* magazine, *National Geographic,* or other picture journals.

10

The way you were

One way to bridge the generation gap is to show your kids that you were a kid once, too. You can prove it by displaying photographs of yourself when you were in elementary school (the same grade as you're teaching, if possible). More exciting, play some old home movies of you as a kid. You might also share some of your favorites from that time—your favorite book, food, game, friend, hobby, song, radio or TV show. Then, as a way of getting acquainted, ask your kids to share some of their favorites.

11

On your marks

In order for kids to see how far they got during this year, they'll need a clear starting point. On day one, have each child contribute to a 9-month time capsule. Contributions can include: height measurements, drawings, samples of printing or handwriting, expectations for the year, voice recordings, the day's newspaper, and other artifacts. Agree with the class that you'll open up the capsule on the last day of school.

12

Sow what?

Bring in a handful of mystery things to plant— big things like bulbs, tiny things like marigold or nasturtium seeds, and even exotic things like Venus-flytrap bulbs (available from seed and garden supply companies). The kids can guess what will come from these seeds. Then plant and hope.

For the longer haul, try planting a seedling that will grow into a large tree as your kids grow up. Depending on your locale and the availability of space, you might try an oak, a maple, or a spruce. Have the kids try to imagine what they'll be doing 25 years in the future when the tree will—with luck—tower over the school building.

13

Guess what?

To add the excitement of mystery to starting-out projects you've planned, conceal items in a large box and invite the kids to "guess what."

The guessing game can be played in several ways. You might have kids try a few and compare the fun and efficiency of the approaches.

• Free-for-all. Kids simply call out their guesses. (Does *anybody* get it?)

• Free-for-all with "getting warmer," "freezing" clues. (Any better luck?)

• Twenty questions, unguided. Kids can ask yes/no questions to get information before registering guesses. (Are kids listening to and learning from the data others discover?)

• Twenty questions, guided. Help kids formulate questions to determine one property of the mystery item—size, color, use—before moving on to something else. (This could be a cooperative effort with a fixed number of questions or a time limit.)

14

Ham it up

Here's one for the real ham—original year-opening song lyrics to be sung to the tune "On Top of Old Smokey." If you can play the piano loudly, you'll probably greatly improve the lyrics:

Hello and how are you?
I hope you are well.
I'm ready to teach you,
How to read and to spell.

That's just the beginning,
So don't take a nap,
I also have lessons,
On reading a map.

And then we'll be zooming,
We'll all be so glad,
That time's still left over,
For numbers to add.

Then multiplication,
Subtraction, too,
Division comes later,
Oh there's so much to do.

I'm expecting a good year,
It'll end much too soon,
We'll have ourselves great fun,
From now until June.

If you get through that one and the kids are still with you, challenge them to write their own lyrics describing their feelings on the first day of school.

15

Ask the kid who was one

Invite one of your former students to visit your class and to describe briefly the things he or she did with you last year. Then let your new kids ask a few questions of their own. Or have a small group of former students make the presentation. It might be less scary to return as a member of a group.

16.

On your question marks

Questions, not answers, are the start of learning. Invite your students to begin the questioning process at the beginning of the year by creating a question bulletin board where students can post their questions. You can start them off with a handful of intriguing questions culled from your curriculum: "How do caterpillars turn into butterflies?" "What makes it rain?" With very young students, you might put a series of puzzling photographs around a giant question mark. Let the students know that you want to hear their questions and that, because their thoughts are important, you will put their questions in a prominent place.

17

Scoop

Invite a local reporter (with photographer) to cover your first day of school. Why *your* class out of all those in your town? "Because," you explain, "we are doing something totally unique, totally newsworthy."

"What," asks the reporter, "are you doing that's so amazing?"

You answer with the unforgettable items you have chosen from this article. If that response doesn't grab the reporter, tell him or her that you're studying key jobs in American life and that you want to start off with the most important of all professionals—the newsperson.

18.

Say it with flowers

Flowers are the traditional bon voyage gift. Why not fill your room with roses, chrysanthemums, daisies and so on as a way of beginning your class's educational voyage? For little kids, the flowers can be the starting point for a first sensory or art lesson.

Murray Suid is a coauthor of *Media and Kids* (Hayden), *Recipes for Writing* (Addison-Wesley), and *The Home of Language Series* (Monday Morning).

Super-duper back-to-school quiz

Directions: Check each question Yes or No.

1. Did you visit any of the following places this summer?
yes (   ) no (   )
  a. the moon
  b. the Land of Oz
  c. dreamland
  d. the local supermarket
  e. a park
  f. any other place
     (explain) _____

2. Did you travel by any of the following means?
yes(   ) no(   )
  a. camel or rickshaw
  b. skateboard or skates
  c. hang glider
  d. roller coaster
  e. foot
  f. other _____

3. Did you talk with any of the following?
yes (   ) no (   )
  a. the President of the U.S.
  b. Mickey Mouse
  c. Santa Claus
  d. a pro baseball player
  e. a relative (uncle, aunt, cousin)
  f. any other interesting person
     _____

4. Did you build any of the following?
yes (   ) no (   )
  a. a rocket ship
  b. a sand castle
  c. a house of cards
  d. a lemonade stand
  e. a friendship
  f. any other thing _____

5. Did you catch any of the following?
yes (   ) no (   )
  a. a butterfly
  b. a thief
  c. a cold
  d. a ball
  e. the wind
  f. any other thing _____

6. Did you get wet in any of the following ways?
yes (   ) no (   )
  a. diving for treasure
  b. riding river rapids
  c. taking a bath or shower
  d. playing with squirt guns
  e. trying to find the end of a rainbow
  f. other _____

7. Did you see any of the following?
yes (   ) no (   )
  a. a shooting star
  b. a movie star
  c. a flying saucer
  d. a concert
  e. an old friend
  f. anything else _____

8. Did you read any of the following?
yes (   ) no (   )
  a. a friend's palm
  b. a wonderful book
  c. the newspaper
  d. a steet sign
  e. a fortune-cookie fortune
  f. anything else _____

9. Did you lose any of the following?
yes (   ) no (   )
  a. your memory
  b. your allowance
  c. your way (how did you get back?)
  d. a fight
  e. a game
  f. a tooth
  g. anything else _____

10. Did you learn any of the following?
yes (   ) no (   )
  a. how to become invisible
  b. how to tie a knot
  c. how to tell time
  d. how to ride a bike
  e. how to throw a curve ball
  f. how to cook an egg (or anything else)
  g. how to do anything else
     _____

11. Did you do anything else you'd like to mention?
yes (   ) no (   )
  a. Mention it here
     _____

How to score your quiz
Give yourself 10 points for each yes.
● If you got 0 to 30 points, you probably slept through most of the summer.
● If you got 40 to 60 points, sounds as if it was a so-so vacation.
● If you got 70 to 90 points, sounds as if things were cooking.
● If you got 100 points or more, sounds—as if you had a good time—just as we'll be having this year.

More grand opening ideas

When the curtain rises on the new school year, greet students with an impressive array of educational showstarters. Made from a few basic materials, these worthy welcoming activities will keep interest in learning high throughout the school year.

Created by *Learning* readers, the following projects are doubly desirable because they contribute to individual students' enthusiasm for school as well as create a sense of class cohesiveness. Among the ideas developed are: a giant grid on which children make their marks, then discuss how they fit in with their classmates; and a birthday recognition system that spotlights celebrants and gives special days a larger context. Other suggestions deal with reading, oral presentations, memory, vocabulary, and special ways to appreciate September and autumn.

Reader of the week

Give oral reading special attention early and often. Announce the Reader of the Week program at the beginning of the year, to encourage students to plan ahead for a moment in the limelight. Each child selects a short book—or a passage in a longer book—to prepare. The goal is to read the selection well and present it to the class. When a reader feels ready, he or she signs up for a time slot.

The audience is also readied through discussions of how to listen appreciatively. Both reader and audience are made aware of such aspects of delivery as volume, inflection, rate, and rapport.

Each Reader of the Week receives a certificate bearing the reader's name, the title and author of the book, and the date of the reading. You may want to display the certificates both to recognize readers' accomplishments and to inspire others in the class. An early start will set the scene for a year of rewarding reading experiences.

Graphic class profile

To give both teacher and children a truly graphic picture of the class makeup, and to inspire a sense of camaraderie right at the start, create a huge graph of the children's vital and not-so-vital statistics.

Prepare a giant grid by numbering the horizontal axis with the number of children in the class. Down the vertical axis write relevant and/or interesting attributes, such as dark haired, left-handed, has a cat, has an older sister, likes pizza, enjoys swimming. Give each student a supply of paper squares of one color, and have students initial each square.

Next, call out each attribute in the form of a question—"How many have an older sister?" Whenever an announced item applies,

	1	**2**
DARK HAIR	T.J.	
LIKES PIZZA		
LEFT-HANDED		
HAS A CAT		
LIKES TO SWIM		
HAS OLDER SISTER		

students affix their squares to the graph.

You may want to allow time for children to discuss their responses, or you may want to use the graph to stimulate discussion at a later time. Either way, it can provide unity-building material for your new class.

Personality-in-the-box

Words may be one way for students to tell about themselves, but student-chosen objects can also reveal a great deal about the members of your new class. Try this start-of-the-year, personality-disclosing activity.

The basic component is an ordinary shoe box covered with brightly colored Con-Tact paper and appropriately decorated. You'll also want to prepare a master of a basic questionaire form, requesting standard name/address/ telephone number/birthdate data, as well as other get-acquainted information: pets, favorites, hobbies, talents, aspirations ("When I grow up, I want to _____"), fantasies ("If I could travel to anywhere in the world, I would go to _____"), etc. For younger children, a note asking for assistance from a helper at home might be in order.

Each day, a different student (or perhaps several if you prepare extra boxes) gets to take the shoe box—with a copy of the questionnaire inside—home. After answering the questions, the child looks for small objects (smaller than a shoe box) that in some way tell about the child's background and personality. Possibilities include: a family photo, a scarf in the child's favorite color, something representative of a favorite food (an empty candy bar wrapper), a roller-skate lace, a postcard from a summer vacation spot, a packet of fish food, a letter from a friend or relative. All chosen items go into the box along with the completed questionnaire.

The following day in school, at a regularly scheduled time, the child exhibits and explains her box-full-of-personal-artifacts. After a brief presentation, the children can exchange questions and answers.

It might be helpful—and serve as a meet-the-teacher introduction as well—if you volunteer to be the first to take the box home and stock it with items indicative of your daily life: a theater-ticket stub, a cartoon that recalls a funny experience you'll explain. By setting an example, you'll not only demonstrate the many possibilities for enclosures and spark ideas, you also may help subsequent shoe-box sharers to participate more comfortably.

First day recap

The first day of school can be so exciting to kids that when asked "What did you do in school today?", many children have a hard time recounting all the goings-on. Wind up that first day—and all other overloaded days of the year as well—in a way that helps children come up with a more accurate response than the ever-popular "Nothing."

A few minutes before day's end, gather the class together for a short recap session of the day's doings. Have them review lessons and recollect experiences in as objective a way as possible. As they do this, ask them to mentally set aside a few nuggets of information that they can easily recall and recount for the at-home audience. These recall items might be ideas or facts from lessons, accounts of new experiences, or getting-along-with-others insights.

Besides being a means of developing better home/school communication, an end-of-day summary session can also be a reminder of goals—and a calming note on which to conclude a busy day, from September to June.

✓ Every-day words

To build kids' vocabularies from the first—and on every—day of school, try a daily program based on a calendar format.

Make a large calendar grid of the month (seven columns, five rows) on tagboard and laminate. With a permanent marker, label the days of the week. Using a water-soluble marker, label the month and insert the month's chosen vocabulary words, distributing them among the grid cells according to the month's configuration of dates.

Next, using construction paper, prepare another grid to mask the word grid. On this grid mark the current month's dates. Cut out each date/cell and attach to the word grid in such a way that each forms a flap that may be opened to reveal a word.

At the beginning of the month, all flaps will be closed, and the grid will look like an ordinary calendar. Each day a flap will be opened to display the word of the day. The procedures for defining, discussing, and practicing the words are up to you and your class.

Birthday wheel

Get-acquainted activities need not—and should not—be crammed into the first week of school. Use birthdays to focus special attention on different students throughout the year. Try a birthday wheel to highlight individuals.

To make the birthday wheel, cut out a large disk from tagboard, divide the disk into 12 sections, and label each section with a month of the year. Write each child's name and birthday in the appropriate section.

The birthday wheel is likely to be a conversation starter right from the beginning. Which month has the greatest number of birthdays? The fewest? Which children are "birthday buddies" with birthdays on the same day or in the same month?

Children whose birthdays fall in September (and perhaps in August as well) start the wheel rolling. Their first task is to bring in and affix small portraits of themselves next to their names on the birthday wheel. Next, they're to begin preparing individual birthday booklets. What kinds of things should a birthday booklet include? Invite suggestions, beginning with these possibilities:

—an account of one or two significant events in your life;

—some favorites: colors, animals, places, sports, teams, books;

—data about the natural world near the time of your birthday (length of the days, flowers in bloom);

—an important event in the news near the time of your birthday;

—a fanciful account of a future birthday: "How I Spent My Twentieth (or Fortieth or Ninetieth) Birthday."

On birthdays (and on assigned alternative days for children whose birthdays occur during summer, on weekends, and on holidays), the birthday child introduces her booklet, perhaps reading selected passages, and attaches it to the birthday wheel with a piece of string for classmates to peruse during free reading times.

Birthdays put the spotlight on the wheel, but you may want to refer to it in-between times to compare nature observations, to update news, or to add a personal (student) perspective to ordinary days.

Soothing jittery nerves

Kids have a lot of first-day anxieties, such as "Where do I sit?" and "What do I do when I get there?" You can help your students get over these anxieties by providing something for each child to read when he first arrives. To find their seats, students look for their names on paper that's on each desk. While they wait for class to begin, they can read what's there, such as Jack Prelutsky's poem "Homework." On the back of the poem, they'll find homework tips for the new year.

Students loosen up with the fun poem and are thankful to have something to occupy them in the first few nervous minutes of class.

Another helpful activity centers on a jigsaw-puzzle bulletin board. First, cut your room number from large sheets of paper. Then, cut the numbers into jigsaw-puzzle–shaped pieces. Students decorate each piece with their name and a drawing or story about themselves, what they did that summer, their favorite book, and so on. The puzzle is then reassembled on the bulletin board, making it clear that everybody's part of the new group.

The ABCs of emotions

Students, especially young ones, may need a rundown on all the different things they're likely to feel during any given school day. To start, read aloud *Feelings Alphabet: An Album of Emotions from A to Z* by Judy Lalli (B.L. Winch and Associates, 1984). Beginning with *afraid*, the book progresses through *curious*, *frustrated*, *silly*, and on to *zonked*. You might remind students that it's okay to feel these things and that they're welcome to come to you with the tough ones (*embarrassed*, *unhappy*, *nervous*, *miserable*).

In your discussion, go back through the alphabet and invite students to think of other emotions beginning with each letter. Can they show each other what these emotions look like? For more on feelings and emotions, introduce students to the book *Feelings* by Aliki (Greenwillow, 1984).

Letter writing

Writing short, personalized notes to your students is a good idea any time of the year. Your students will appreciate the individual attention and the chance to get to know you on an informal basis.

Place a short note on each student's desk the first day of school. You might introduce yourself and give a few details about your life outside of school—the name of your dog, your favorite ice cream, and so on. The letter can end with something such as:

> I'll be writing each of you now and then during the school year, and I'd love it if you'd write back. Today, for instance, I'd like to know a couple of things about you. Will you drop me a note?
>
> Fondly,

It may take time for some students to warm up to note-passing with a teacher, but the fun of getting letters may outweigh their reluctance. You can use the notes to give special encouragement, to inquire if a troubled student wants to talk, or so on.

What's in a name?

While students are learning new names and faces, ask them why they think people have last names. Did they always? What would it be like if they didn't?

Invite students to think of categories of names and choose one or two to focus on as a class. They might choose occupation names (Baker, Taylor, Warden); landscape names (Meadows, Fields, Rivers); or names that at one time described people (Stout, Long, Wise, Swift). Encourage them to try offbeat categories as well. (In *A Book About Names* [Crowell, 1984], author Milton Meltzer tried this activity with the category *fish*. He gathered from phone books and other sources the names Bass, Pike, Oyster, Trout, Mullet, Sole, Salmon, and Goldfisch.)

Write the categories you've chosen on the board, and list names students have heard of or read about in books.

Reading about friends

To help students adjust to the ups-and-downs of friendship that can characterize the beginning of the school year, fill your shelves and tabletops with fiction on the subject. For example, young children might enjoy *Lizzie and Harold* by Elizabeth Winthrop (Lothrop, Lee and Shepard, 1985). In this book, Lizzie searches far and wide for a best friend, only to find that Harold's been there all along.

You might read the books aloud or have them on hand for students to choose from during free reading time. If you need suggestions, check your library for *The Bookfinder: When Kids Need Books* by Sharon Spredemann Dreyer (American Guidance Service, 1985). This book provides detailed annotations on hundreds of children's books and indexes them by subject.

Sing-along

Use a special version of the song "Camptown Races" to welcome your students back to school. For example, first-grade children learn the words:

The first-grade chil-
   dren sing their song,
Doo-dah! doo-dah!
The first-grade chil-
   dren dance along,
Oh! doo-dah day!

Come down the hall
   with smiles on,
Doo-dah! doo-dah!
Find a chair to sit right
   on,
Oh! doo-dah day!

Chorus:
Goin' to sing all night!
Goin' to sing all day!
I bet my money on a
   violin,
Your goin' to like your
   stay!

Next, students draw their own faces on oaktag musical notes that are then arranged on bulletin board staffs complete with lines, treble clefs, and so on. The title of the bulletin board? "Sing a Song of Children."

Celebrate September

Get off to a good start by sharing with your students how special September is. Autumn begins in September; we honor workers on Labor Day, the first Monday of the month; and two Jewish holidays—Rosh Hashanah and Yom Kippur—frequently fall during the last days of the month. Following are more September events, along with suggestions for observing them. Some of the activities might become an ongoing part of the year's curriculum.

What's in a name?

The word *Kodak,* the story goes, was as meaningless as a child's first *goo* when George Eastman registered it on September 4, 1888, as the name for his roll-film camera, the first ever patented. The word, said Eastman, "snaps like a camera shutter in your face. What more can one ask?" You might consider letting children record the year's highlights with photographs.

Ask children to compile a list of trade names and to speculate on their origins and on the messages they're meant to convey. Then have them write business letters inquiring about the most intriguing of these trade names (being sure to follow up with thank-you letters).

Stories in rhyme

Legend has it that General "Stonewall" Jackson ordered his soldiers to fire on the Union flag flying in Barbara Fritchie's attic window on September 6, 1862. This alleged Civil War incident was the basis for John Greenleaf Whittier's poem "Barbara Fritchie." Read this story poem to your class and provide books of collected story poems for students to read on their own. Encourage children to read and discuss them with classmates. Ask each child to choose at least one favorite to share with the class.

Watch your words

An American meat packer announced, on September 10, 1927, the production of a frankfurter that came in a unique "zippered casing." Customers were instructed to "boil the hot dog in its zippered casing and then discard it." Do these instructions say what they mean? Ask students to be on the lookout for the other slipups in the use of our language and to collect them for a class scrapbook. Also include sections in the scrapbook for samples of clever and imaginative uses of words. *A Children's Almanac of Words at Play* by William R. Espy (Crown, 1983) should help enliven interest in words and their use.

World of wonder

Michael Faraday, whose scientific discoveries laid the groundwork for the age of electricity, was born on September 22, 1791. He believed his role as a scientist was to increase humankind's understanding of the world; through his many experiments, he succeeded in fulfilling that role.

From childhood, Michael Faraday was a questioner, wondering about nearly everything he saw. Using Faraday as a model, encourage children to question the things they see and to tell about their questions. Make a list of their questions. Use this list as a guide to planning units, to carrying out experiments, and as a source of topics for independent research.

To get children started wondering and experimenting, pose these questions, which Faraday asked during one of his series of children's lectures, this one titled "The Chemical History of a Candle": What makes a candle burn? Why is the flame brighter at the top? Why does a candle's light go out if you put it under a jar? Where does a candle go when it burns? If possible, have on hand a copy of *Coils, Magnets, and Rings: Michael Faraday's World* by Nancy Veglahn (Coward, 1976).

Dear pen pal

September 22, 1694, was the birthday of Philip Dormer Stanhope, the Earl of Chesterfield. He was an English writer and statesman, who became famous for his letters to his son. These letters were published in 1774 and are still considered models in the art of letter writing.

Early in the year, involve your children in writing letters to pen pals. The class should decide whether to write to children in other states or countries in hopes of learning about different ways of life, or whether to exchange letters with a nearby class with which it might be possible to get together during the year.

Seed harvest

Fall begins on or about September 21. The harvest season is a good time for collecting seeds. Ask children to gather a variety of them from home and outdoors and to sort them in different ways—by size, shape, color. Then have them make displays of the different seed categories.

Collect the blossoms-gone-to-seed from several plants of the same species—perhaps goldenrod or sunflowers. Figure out as closely as possible the number of seeds each plant has produced. Using these statistics, compute the average number of seeds per plant. If one square foot of land were allowed for each seed, how much land would be required to sow the seeds produced by just one of these plants? Would the school playground be large enough to hold them? Discuss why it's necessary for plants to make so many seeds.

For an autumn treat, sprout mung beans or alfalfa seeds and use them in sandwiches. And for more fun with seeds, play this game. Throw two or three milkweed seeds into the air, and see how long students can keep them aloft by blowing them.

Sandra Nye is an elementary school teacher in West Babylon, N.Y., and a consultant with Marilyn Burns Education Associates.

Fire drills—Do they prepare you for the real thing?

In the stress and strain of the average class-room teacher's day, fire drills get about the same serious attention as, say, a garden club tea. But they deserve serious attention when you're planning procedures for the school year.

The fact is, however, that major fires are by no means something that will always occur in somebody else's school. Statistically speaking, the odds are about one in six that a fire large enough to threaten lives and property will occur in any given school in any given year. With the safety and welfare of children at stake, there is a clear necessity for drills to move higher on most school priority lists.

If a serious fire does start in your school, your students may have only a few minutes to escape. Those few minutes will require clear thinking by both you and your children. Unfortunately, most school fire drills do not improve the chances of that happening.

Drills that don't matter

We teachers usually know the drill is coming and are therefore seldom genuinely startled. Even very young children soon discover that drills almost always come on nice days, usually just before or after recess or lunch, or during music or art, "which don't really matter much anyway." They are equally aware that we teachers aren't alarmed, and, in fact, miraculously manage to have a sweater handy if it's brisk outside.

The drills always go smoothly. All doors are open and halls clear. Everyone marches out obediently, reassured by the clear understanding that it's all a put-up job.

These drills are well intentioned, make everyone feel more secure, and satisfy the fire marshal and the insurance carrier. But they do not equip you or your students to respond properly in a real fire.

To make emergency drills more helpful, create the conditions that would be present in a genuine emergency, and teach both children and teachers how to deal with them realistically.

Real fires don't invariably occur on good-weather days—and neither should drills. Of course we must be concerned about the weather's effect on children's health, but if drills are conducted as efficiently as they should be, everyone will be out and back very quickly. Nor is it necessary to choose a 20-below-zero day to meet the criterion of reality.

But what do we do if the weather is very bad and we have a real fire? If we never drill on such days, we will never discover either the problems or their solutions. We might never discover, for example, that for short periods, or in only moderately cold weather, teachers can keep children adequately warm by leading them in "jumping jacks" or other calisthenics. It might also make good sense to ask school architects to sacrifice aesthetics and make it possible for children to hang their coats on open pegs so that they can pick them up as they go by, much as firemen do. How much better is that arrangement than having children outside coatless, perhaps being sprayed by fire hoses, in freezing temperatures.

In the event of a real fire, do you know where the fire trucks are likely to be located in the schoolyard? Ask the fire department to show you, then rearrange exit lines so children are not in that area or in any other dangerous traffic areas. You may be surprised to discover that some of your present room lines are assigned to just such areas.

Should children get farther from the building than they do in the average drill to be safe from water, heat, or falling debris? If so, there should be a second signal—perhaps four short bells—indicating that you should lead your class 200 feet or more from the school.

Plan for emergency shelter

Would children have to go to other buildings or nearby homes for shelter? Have you located the space and trained the volunteers? Have you an external signal that would alert volunteer neighborhood mothers to get ready for the children sent to their homes for shelter by turning off stoves, securing dangerous pets, and putting babies in protected places.

Have you a bullhorn or other means of giving directions to the children standing outside? Where is it stored? Whoever in your school is responsible for overall direction of the fire protection program should carry this equipment on all drills.

In a real emergency, wouldn't you expect at least some minor mishaps—scrapes, cuts, burns? Does the school nurse have an emergency kit, a fast way to move it, and an established location outside so teachers and children know where to find her? And does she take her equipment on all drills?

Will parents panic and race to the scene? Is anyone assigned to control traffic, to let the media know what's happening, and to urge parents not to come?

A real fire might start when everyone is in the gym or the lunch room, so some drills should start there, too. Since teachers wouldn't know about a fire in advance, they should not be informed of drills in advance. We all need practice in reacting without either prior notice

or panic. At least a few drills should be called by an outside administrator so that the principal, too, has a chance to test his or her reactions to an emergency.

Obviously, in a real fire everyone must leave the building. In drills, many teachers stay in the warm building or huddle just inside or outside the door—urging the kids to go on out. Do the custodians, secretaries and cooks follow drills, or are they made of asbestos? All school personnel should be required to leave and go the required distance from the building during a drill, cold or hot, rainy or dry.

Consider smoke, sick children, and showers

In a real fire, there will be smoke, blocked exits, and general confusion. Everyone should know alternative ways out of the building. Every once in a while, a harmless smoke device should be used, or a barricade should block a familiar exit. An even simpler way to simulate obstacles is suitable for younger children. Immediately after the siren, the principal might simply announce on the public address system that the east hallway is blocked at Room 7 or some other spot. This will require children and teachers to think quickly and clearly. It will also point up procedures that need change or more practice.

We regularly allow sick children to stay in the nurse's office during drills in bad weather because we do not wish to expose them to the elements. In a real fire they would have to leave, so prepare for it by having enough blankets to wrap them in, and take them out.

A fire may start when older students are in the pool or the showers. Is there a procedure for getting them out without waiting to dress? Maybe blankets are one answer—but there had better be an answer. Until schools start holding genuine and serious drills, no one will even realize there is a question.

In a large school, be sure students know all the teachers and staff on sight or issue emergency identification badges so that everyone knows whose directions are to be followed. Whenever a substitute is assigned, the teacher next door should be responsible for being sure the substitute knows how to proceed.

Children should be trained both to leave quickly and quietly and to remain quiet outdoors so that directions and messages can be heard. Then, when the all clear sounds, sing, dance or yell your way back into the school. If the drill has been taken seriously, the tension level needs to be lowered. This device serves the additional purpose of demonstrating that rules of silence are not made just for the nasty fun of ordering kids around, that they are imposed only when really needed.

Children who are likely to panic or to suffer seizures or serious respiratory problems if exposed to smoke should be identified in advance. A simple "roller" desk chair can be used to move a child who faints or the awkward kid wearing a leg cast.

In smoky fires, the buddy system and human chains save lives. But they won't help unless you practice them. All teachers should be sure they know at least three alternative exists from their own classrooms. Moreover, they should practice getting out of them blindfolded, first because that roughly approximates the visibility level when smoke is heavy, and second because it leaves a strong impression of the genuine dangers and our responsibility to react to them properly.

Every fire signal, like every report of a suicide attempt, must be assumed to be real. Repeated sloppy, put-on drills can only make children less able to handle genuine emergencies—perhaps even less able than if there had been no drills at all.

So get your fire chief to help you plan drills. If you contact him and make it possible for him to do so at a convenient time, his department may actually arrive and lay out some hoses and follow other "real-fire" procedures. It's good practice for the firemen and a fine opportunity for the children to observe the serious and efficient behavior required in an emergency situation. Remember that these procedures apply equally well to bomb threats, gas or fume dangers, floods, earthquakes, or any other emergencies that require clearing the building quickly.

It is not a big job to check procedures and plan for safe practices. Perhaps the PTA will volunteer to contact nearby parents and recruit them to open their homes, help supervise children, direct traffic and the like, in case of a fire. They might also locate all the phones in the immediate neighborhood that householders are willing to let proper school personnel use. Every teacher should have the parents' name, address, and telephone number for everyone in his or her class, a similar staff list and a list of emergency telephone numbers.

By all means let the children in on the planning. They'll have good ideas, and their participation in the planning will help them to understand how vital it is to take all fire drills very seriously. And you will find that this exercise will inspire them to help make safety plans for the family at home.

The fire alarm is always a chilling sound. But if your school has good emergency procedures and realistic drills, it need never signal a real tragedy.

Jean Gatch is a free-lance writer and has taught in elementary through college levels, including teacher training and experimental programs.

2
HELP STUDENTS GET ACQUAINTED

As an experienced teacher, you've learned to overcome the anxieties that go with facing a room full of children you've never seen before. But for students, overcoming the anxiety of dealing with the new and unfamiliar—new teacher, new classmates, new school, perhaps even a new community—is often difficult. Anything you can do to ease their adjustment and hasten their sense of belonging to the learning community that meets in your classroom is sure to help you establish a positive climate. You're sure to find some practical ideas in the following classroom-tested activities.

Meeting new faces

New faces, friendly faces, hard-to-read faces, growing-up faces—are you ready to face them all? Will you manage to master the names and discover the personalities that go with them?

A face that's a moving target is tough to study. Not so a photograph. The following classroom-tested photo projects can help you become familiar with the sea of faces you'll soon be encountering. They'll also help students get acquainted with one another, the school staff, the new year—and even with themselves.

Library book IDs

Try this easy-to-do photo project: making personalized bookmarks. Small school portraits are perfect for these, or ask children to bring in their favorite snapshots (ones that can be cut up). You could also bring in a camera and take the photos yourself.

Distribute tagboard or sturdy paper, scissors, paste, and pencils or markers. Have each child cut a strip of tagboard about 1½″ wide, then paste his or her photo, which has been trimmed to fit the bookmark width, in place at one end of the strip. The rest of the strip can be decorated in any way the child chooses, including printing or writing the child's name down the length of the bookmark, creating monograms, drawing a self-portrait, or making a statement about books or reading, such as "Pat Palmer says, 'Books are beautiful!' " Then the personalized bookmark can be slipped inside the child's current library book—for instant identification.

Photo cards for class activities

Making a set of student photo cards can be useful in a variety of individual and small-group activities. (If you're able to make photo cards of teachers and other staff members, you can expand the content of the photo card tasks.)

Mount a photo of each child on an index card and laminate or cover with clear Con-Tact paper. If you wish, write the child's name on the card with a pencil or wash-off marker. These labels should be removed as soon as the children have learned one another's names.

The children can then use the photo cards for the following tasks:

• *Ordinal photos.* Select five or more photos and prepare a direction card giving the order in which the photo cards are to be placed in a chalk tray. For example:

third	....	John
fifth	....	Sue
second	....	Beth
first	....	George
fourth	....	Scott

• *Initial match.* Prepare a set of "initials only" cards—one card for each child's initials. Children may then match photo cards and initial cards as a game or as an independent activity.

• *Personality quiz.* Compose pocket chart sentences to be completed by adding appropriate photos:

> *Two girls with rhyming names are* (PHOTO) *and* (PHOTO).
> *Three children who wear glasses are* (PHOTO), (PHOTO), *and* (PHOTO).
> *Our school nurse is* (PHOTO).

• *Math picture problems.* Write math problems using the names of children in the class. Children then solve the problems and display correct "answer photos":

> *Mark, Louise, and Steven were playing Frisbee. Then Mark had to go home. How many children were left playing Frisbee?*
> *Answer: 3 − 1 = 2 (Louise's photo) (Steven's photo)*

• *Alphabetical order.* Distribute photo cards to each of four children. Then have children arrange all the photos in an alphabetically ordered row by first names (or last names), calling out the name as each photo is placed.

• *Alike and different.* Have a child choose two photos and then write one sentence that tells something about how the two children are the same, and one sentence telling how they are different.

Once you've made a set of photo cards, you'll probably discover many more uses for them.

This is where Dorothy lives

Children's photos can help accomplish a major kindergarten objective: having children learn their names and addresses.

Begin by preparing construction-paper cutouts of simple house shapes—one house per child—and staple the houses to a bulletin board entitled, "I Know My Name and Address."

You'll also need a closeup photo of each child. You might start taking the photos early in preparation for the project, or you can schedule this activity after the school pictures are taken.

As soon as a child can give her full name and street address or rural route, invite her to pick out a house. The house is then prepared for occupancy. Cut out a doorway and over the top of the door print the child's name. To the side of the doorway, write the child's address.

Each child will be eager to "own" his own house—and thus be motivated to master the name-and-address objective of the activity—so don't be surprised if your bulletin-board village is completely occupied within a couple of weeks. It's a real image booster for young children to see themselves "standing in their doorways," and a good way for visitors to the class to get acquainted with your students.

The dynamic duo, the terrific twosome

Here's a way of making the mandatory sharing of lockers a more positive experience, with smiles all around.

As soon as students have chosen locker partners, plan a snapshot session. Take a picture of each pair of partners, with the pose open to whatever theatrics the two decide on—tempered, perhaps, by the reminder that the photo will be on display on their locker all year long.

When all of the locker partners have been photographed and the pictures processed, mount each photo on a colorful construction-paper background and cover with clear Con-Tact paper. Then hang the photos on the lockers for all to admire and enjoy throughout the year.

Your mini-"rogues' gallery" of comical pairs is sure to be a hit, as well as an effective locker identification system.

School welcome album

A student-prepared "Welcome to Our School" album full of photos can be a useful orientation for new students throughout the year. (If you have a copying machine that reproduces photos clearly, you can make several albums; if not, a single class album will suffice.)

First, have students research and list the people who make up the school staff: teachers; the principal; secretaries; librarian; cafeteria; custodial and medical personnel; etc. Next, arrange photo-taking sessions with these persons in their "native environments." Include one or more students from the class in each photo. Photograph classroom activities and playground scenes as well. You might also include photos to introduce newcomers to the building itself.

When the picture-taking is completed, students can make their choices of photos to be featured in the album. Students then write a one-line caption for each photo, introducing the staff person or activity being shown.

The next step calls for creativity and a sense of humor. Students imagine conversations among the characters shown in the photos and put the words into comic-strip-style speech balloons cut from plain paper and pasted onto the photos.

When all the photo pages have been laid out and assembled, students can prepare a preface explaining the purpose of the album and telling how it was created. Acknowledgements might be included, and of course, a suitably intriguing cover will need to be designed. The album is then ready for browsing by new students and perhaps by parents attending open house.

Later the welcome album can serve as a springboard to conversation writing: students incorporate the speech-balloon messages into connected prose—with *said*s and quotation marks in place.

Creating the album may alert students to other areas of the curriculum that could be enriched with "photocomics"—and put the class on the trail of further photo projects.

Discovering who's who and keeping the whos sorted out—with each personality firmly established—can be an easier task when photo projects are part of the school start-up scene. And through the year, as you glance at Todd and T.J. hamming it up on their locker door or glimpse Cindy's proud smile on the bookmark inside her favorite book on wolves, you'll be reminded of the unique individuals that make up this year's brand-new gallery of faces.

10 ways to help new kids feel at home

Every year it happens: you, as a teacher, face children you've never set eyes on before. You've learned to deal with the anxieties that can produce, especially if you've been teaching for a number of years. After all, you know the school and its procedures, and as an adult, you've developed the skills to meet new situations. But many of the children are typically much less confident. Their lack of experience in dealing with change leaves them vulnerable and uncomfortable in unfamiliar surroundings. Kids who have done no more than change teachers or classes within a school often have a difficult time, and kids new to a school and a community find the transition even harder.

In our mobile society, some six million children move to a new community each year. If these kids are to learn to cope with moving, they are likely to need more than the help of their parents, who may be unprepared themselves or too burdened with their own adjustments to give their children the necessary support. Kids, therefore, need the help of the teachers and students in their new school.

The transition is easiest for kids who are in a classroom where the students and teacher get along well, respect each other and themselves, and feel they are part of a learning community. Developing this kind of atmosphere is no easy job, especially at the start of the new school year. No single method will establish an ideal environment, but you can help new students in your class feel at home by these practical suggestions for activities that help smooth the transition.

GETTING ACQUAINTED ACTIVITIES

1
Picture box

This is a nonthreatening and enjoyable way to get to know a child. Ask the new child if she would like to sort through a box of pictures with you to find a selection that will help her make up a story. While looking through the box, children usually talk freely about themselves. The interest you show and the responses you give to her comments will help lay the groundwork for mutual trust. It will also give you some indications about her personality and capabilities.

Once she selects the pictures, have her write a story or dictate one to you. If you think that sharing the story with the rest of the class will focus positive attention on the new student, ask her if she would like to read it to the class or if she will permit you to read it. And if she doesn't want it to be read, see if she would mind having it posted.

2
Select-a-friend

Once you know something about the child personally, you will want to see how she relates to her peers and what type of child she likes best. Find out if she would like to work with you and another student of her own choosing on a special, pleasant project—cooking or decorating a wall or a corner of the room. While working with the pair, you will have a chance to observe them and facilitate their interaction.

3

Parent involvement

To add both to the new child's sense of belonging and your own sense of the child, encourage her parents to participate in some way in school activities. One way is to initiate a party or picnic that parents, including the new child's, can help organize. By planning the event themselves, parents will have a chance to communicate directly with one another instead of through you. Usually when parents begin to feel accepted in the community, so do their children.

At the party or at individual or group conferences with the parents of new children, try to find out as much as possible about each new student. Parents are usually happy to talk about their children and reassured to learn that you want to treat kids as individuals. Knowing something about the student—she is the youngest sibling or is afraid to try new math concepts—will help you deal more effectively with her. These conferences can lay the foundation for effective cooperation between home and school.

Pairs. Pair students off and encourage them to exchange names and bits of information about themselves. If you have an odd number of students, include yourself in the activity. Each pair then meets with another pair, and the partners introduce each other as fully as possible. Then the foursome meets with another foursome and repeats the procedure. (Variation: After two pairs have exchanged information, organize the kids into new pairs.) When the game is finished, have the information written up and mimeographed as your "This is Us" booklet. Make enough copies for the entire class.

Questions. To solicit information beyond what the students might come up with themselves, write questions on the board and then pair the children up to discuss them. During the discussion each member of the pair takes notes on the other's answers. These notes can be used in a class discussion and in compiling the "This is Us" booklet. A few suggested questions: "What is the funniest experience you ever had? The saddest?" "What was your strangest dream?" "Who in your life has had the most influence on you?" "Who was your favorite teacher? Why?" "Where is the best place you have ever been?"

4

This is Us

Making a "This is Us" booklet of the names, addresses, and phone numbers of both you and the students is a good way for everyone to become acquainted. The booklet should be updated throughout the year to include changing information about both old and new students. The booklet can be produced through one or both of the following activities:

5

Creative activities

If you find that the new student isn't at ease during regular academic activities and you haven't yet introduced creative expression, now is a good time to do so. Dance, drama, music, art, or poetry may uncover talents that you can use as another bridge between her and the class.

6
Class interview

A technique for focusing on an individual in helping others get to know her is the class interview. In one type of interview, the whole class prepares questions from which a panel of five reporters selects several to ask the new student. The new child has the option of choosing a host who will introduce her before and sit next to her during the interview. As an alternative to the class interview, you can reverse the procedure and have the new child play the role of roving reporter. Given note pad and pencil or tape recorder and a couple of weeks to collect information, your young Barbara Walters can go about interviewing each of her new classmates. The activity finale can take a "Guess who I'm describing?" form—the interviewer reveals information gathered in the interview without revealing the student's name. Each class member tries to identify the mystery student.

7
Home-school map

Develop a map, with the kids if possible, clearly indicating home locations in relationship to the school and to each other. Bus routes and transportation methods between various locations can be penciled in during a map-study discussion. Neighborhood, class-time, or after-school walks can yield a feeling of familiarity and solidarity in and outside the classroom. When new students arrive during the year, take out the map for updating.

8
Big siblings

Organize a Big Siblings Club for your school. Ask help from older kids and faculty advisors in planning ways to make new, younger students feel at home in the school. One way is to match up a Big Sibling with one or more younger students who live near each other or who are in the same homeroom. Kick off the program with a party for the entire group by inviting other teachers, the principal, and parents.

Big Siblings can also be used as peer counselors. Trained by counselors in the school, the Big Siblings should be prepared to listen well and talk straight to the kids who come to them for advice or a friendly ear.

9
Sponsors

Within your class, form a group of kids who are thoroughly familiar with the school and the community. Let them plan ways to make new members of the class feel welcome. The sponsors can advise the newcomers about class and school rules and schedules, accompany them to and from school, and spend time with them during lunch and recesses—the periods when new students are most often alone.

10
I'm unique

The activities already suggested are good starting points for integrating the new child. To ensure even greater acceptance, communication must be extended beyond introductory exercises. Now that you and the class know about each other, find a way to focus positively on something you have learned about the new child and to which the other children can relate. For instance, if the child is from another part of your state or the country, she could tell about the things that are unique to that area. Activities and discussions involving differences may arise from such a presentation. In addition, if a new student has a special skill or talent—being expert at making paper airplanes or doing long division—find a way to share her abilities with the class.

Watch for special problems

Some new-kid problems don't surface during regular class time. If you're willing to share part of your lunch, recess, or planning time with the class, you're likely to uncover some of these hidden problems. By discovering and dealing with them early, you'll save time and energy in the long run.

More readily identifiable problems, such as hostility, rejection, or ostracism of newcomers, can be dealt with through role playing or problem-solving discussions. Exercise your own judgment as to whether the entire class or only those students most closely involved should participate. You can assign parts in such a way that students find themselves in unaccustomed roles. If ostracism is a problem, try this role-playing situation: Have four shy children pretend they are involved in a game with which they are familiar. Have a new child, played by a class leader, pretend she wants to join the game but is shy and does not know all the rules. Tell all the participants that the "new kid," though afraid of rejection, wants to play the game, but the other four children

are reluctant to let her in. Then have them spontaneously act out the drama. A discussion of how it feels to be new, to be rejected and to reject follows naturally from the role play.

Sharing your own feelings and interpretations is also effective. One way is to describe how you felt when you were rejected or felt alone. You can use yourself as a model as soon as a problem arises or later, during a class or group meeting. By telling how you dealt with a situation, you may enlarge each child's repertoire of coping mechanisms. Children are often relieved to learn that adults have suffered just as they have. Moreover, being in touch with your own feelings of rejection will probably enable you to be more spontaneous and empathetic in helping the new child.

Clarification and feedback

You will regularly want to assess how well new children are adapting. The best guideline is your own observation. But other measures can help. Though a child may appear to be adjusting well in school, she may be having problems at home. For example, a child who gets along well with classmates at school may act depressed at home because her friendships don't extend beyond the classroom. The best way to obtain this kind of information is through conferences with both students and parents after the initial adjustment to the school has passed. You can alleviate the problem of kids being lonely at home by giving parents class enrollment lists with telephone numbers and addresses. Parents can then help their kids get in touch with classmates outside the school.

Help students who must move

Some of the problems with new students might

have been prevented or ameliorated had the students been better prepared before moving. If you know in advance that one of your students is going to leave, you can help reduce her anxieties. She can be given an individual or group study project to find out about the area to which she will be moving. Another step is to hold a group discussion about how it feels to move, drawing especially upon those students who have recently made moves themselves. Before the child leaves, the class can think of ways to keep in touch—through class letters or cassette messages. The kids might develop this into a pen-pal exchange after the student is established in her new school. The possibility of visits should also be explored.

Moving is almost always a wrench for kids, and no panacea for the pain exists. But teachers can be instrumental in making such adjustments easier. (Classroom activities help make the new student more comfortable, but what ultimately makes her feel she belongs is knowing that you and her classmates accept her as a unique individual.)

Mary Grishaver, a former classroom teacher and a poet and psychologist, was a free-lance writer at original publication of this article. Her coauthor, **Bruce Raskin,** was a staff editor for *Learning* magazine.

FIRST-DAY GUIDEBOOK

As you think ahead to that always-important first day with your new class, consider providing each student with an orientation guide to ease the settling-in process. Put yourself in the place of the "new kid" and imagine the kinds of information that could be helpful to have in hand—and to take home—right away.

For a start, the guidebook's cover—in addition to welcoming the student to your class—could carry such basics as the school name, the school address and phone number, the classroom number, and your name.

Inside, you might include:
—a staff directory that introduces the principal, the secretary, the nurse, the nutritionist, the custodian, etc.;
—a simplified floor plan of the school (which could come in handy for map study later on);
—listings of school calendar dates and events—holidays, conference days, vacations,
etc. (and perhaps an occasional just-for-fun celebration);
—a sample daily schedule (subject to all kinds of changes, of course);
—a sneak preview of unit topics likely to be covered during the year;
—a brief statement on classroom policy and procedures (written in as nonthreatening a way as possible).

You might also include sev-
eral blank pages on which students can write the names and telephone numbers of classmates, as well as record personal reminders and notes.

A first-day guidebook can not only help newcomers get a better start; with a few imaginative touches, the book can be an enjoyable reference throughout the year.

Getting acquainted and getting together

Step right up, teachers! It's September! It's back-to-school time! Step a little closer. Get a glimpse of those kids! Shiny shoes, fresh shirts, new pencils, still with erasers! They're ready! They're eager! But inside they're a bit cautious—a little suspicious about that first day back. Not wanting to be disappointed. Not wanting to write that composition about summer vacation. Not wanting that same old stuff!

What do do? Try these fabulous, fantastic ideas. They're practical! Down to earth! Simple to do! Easy to prepare! Guaranteed for getting acquainted!

Getting kids to work together

When you send two children off to work together, do they wind up talking about everything but their work? Arguing over pencils, discussing lunch, getting noisier and noisier? You do want them to have the opportunity to learn about each other. What do you do? Try the following "Stuff to do with a Partner":

1. Look at each other and list your similarities and differences. Don't sneak a peek at your partner's list while you do it.

2. Next, without looking at your partner, draw a picture of her. Put it in a safe place.

3. Now you get to draw another picture looking at your partner. You can both do this at the same time.

4. Show your pictures to your friend. Can she tell which one you drew first?

5. What did you see *without* looking that you didn't see when you looked? Which picture tells more about your partner? Which picture of yourself do you like best? Which does your friend like? Look at the pictures other kids drew of each other.

6. Collaborate on a book. Include the portraits. Write about your pictures. Write a letter to your friend about her pictures.

7. Write a story... "Who I look like most in my class, and why."

Pulling together as a group

To get kids to work towards a close, group feeling, start off by brainstorming ideas together to develop Classstuff—like a class cheer, class colors, a secret class handshake, a class flower, or a class guestbook.

Tricks with twine

Try Penelope Bodyparts' fantastic tricks using only her body and a piece of twine.

1. Penelope cuts a piece of twine longer than she is tall.

2. Now Penelope measures around her wrist from one end of the string, then she carefully ties a knot—and there's her wrist measurement!

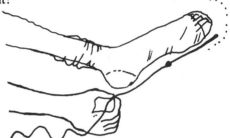

3. On to her foot. Again she measures from the same end of the string, toe to heel, and ties a knot. Show us what you've got now, Penelope.

4. Up to her head, around, ties a knot—good!

5. Waist next...

6. And her height. A friend helps out. And here it is. Penelope's Knotted Measures! Why Penelope, it looks like your height is 3 times your head.

All right, class. You try it now. Try this... Find out how many of your widest smiles make your height. Guess first, then use your string. When you're finished, can you find anyone with a string knotted just like yours?

And when you try this with the little ones, have them measure fewer things and mark the string with crayon or markers instead of tying knots.

Sharing how you feel

We give clues about ourselves in lots of ways other than talking—our clothes, the expressions on our faces, how we walk, what we're carrying, and so forth. Imagine Mr. Al K. Seltzer, who has a cold. What does his appearance tell about how he feels? Now how about someone trying this. Come up and *without saying anything* show us how you feel about being here today. We have lots to learn about each other—and that means keeping our eyes, our ears, and our minds open.

That's it, teachers! Let these ideas get you started and keep you going. We want those kids to WORK together, LEARN together, HUM together, STRUM together. That means learning about each other. And that starts from learning about themselves. It all has to do with celebrating our differences—and that's what will get your class together!

Marilyn Burns is the author and **Martha Weston** is the illustrator of nine books for children, including *The I Hate Mathematics! Book, The Book of Think,* and *I Am Not a Short Adult!* Martha has also illustrated Marilyn's latest book for teachers, *A Collection of Math Lessons.*

LIKE, UNLIKE, UNIQUE

Here's a little different way of playing the "getting-to-know-you" game. In this one, everyone gets to hear everyone else say something, but no one needs to feel the pressure of self-consciousness.

Pair up students for introduction interviews. The goal of each pair's discussion is to come up with: (1) something they have in common, (2) something they disagree about, and (3) something each feels might be unique about his or her partner.

Provide for about five minutes of interview time. If you sense difficulty in getting started, you might suggest categories such as: things you enjoy eating, special sounds, things you like to look at; favorite song or musical group, favorite TV show or sport (or most *disliked* in these categories); most memorable memory; nickname; most effective time waster; ambitions, dreams, etc.

To facilitate reporting (making introductions) later on, students can jot down what they'd like to say about their partners in the three categories of likenesses, differences, and uniqueness.

After the interview period, call on pairs to introduce each other to the class. It might begin like this:

"Hi, I've been talking to Sandy Shaw. She and I both are only children and both of us were born in June. Sandy really loves pizza, but I'm a chocolate freak. The thing about Sandy that's unique is that she lived in India for five years."

"OK, this is Greg Daniels. He and I both hate alarm clocks and love big dogs. Greg's best subject is history, but I like science. He's a tennis nut and he's probably the only one in the class who ruined three rackets last summer."

You might schedule the introductions over three or four sessions to help ensure that no speaker will go up against an audience with "24-down-and-6-to-go" fidgets.

Paired introductions help each student to become somewhat knowledgeable about one other class member—beyond the brief bits that everyone will be hearing. And the introductions may prime the class as a whole for discussion of diversity and uniqueness (which may

lead even further to consideration of values and self-concept explorations).

Shortly after the introductions, you might ask students' names and one thing that was said about each. It might be interesting to see what sorts of things people are most apt to remember.

Another angle on memory: In setting up the introduction activity, you might ask students to try to come up with memory-aiding gimmicks to go along with their names. Suggest that the gimmicks be something they'd *like* to be associated with, as well as something that sticks in people's minds—so they won't forever afterward have to put up with "silly Sally" or "Fred the red."

GETTING-TO-KNOW-YOU BINGO

This personalized variation of Bingo is a great ice breaker during the first weeks of school. Instead of numbers, characteristics or information relating to the students fill the squares and children must ask each other questions to win the game.

Make a duplicating master of a Bingo card—five rows across, five down—and fill each block with a few words that describe a student in your class. (If you have more than 25 students, you'll need a bigger grid—5 by 6, or whatever is necessary.) Records can give you some information; simple observation,

of course, can tell you who "has freckles," "has red hair," "likes to wear purple." You might also have heard about a student who "took a trip to Mexico this summer" or who "has a new baby brother." Whatever positive details you use, be sure to include each student in at least one block. You might also consider including a few facts about yourself so that students can get to know you as well as one another.

When the card has been filled, make copies and distribute them to the children. Players must now find the kids who

fit the descriptions. When they find the boy with red hair or the girl who has a new brother, they must ask the child to sign the appropriate space on the card. The game ends when you call time or when a student has all the squares of his card signed. Winners are those with the most signatures.

This game can get noisy, but the lively interchanges can set the tone for a positive year together.

3

GET GOING WITH COOPERATION

Helping students to learn to work together successfully is vitally important. Much more than a technique that leads to easier classroom management, it's a means of promoting interaction among students; thus, it also serves their intellectual development. The following articles offer practical ideas for encouraging cooperation through various games and a method of grouping you can try in your own classroom.

Groups of four: Solving the management problem

Every September for years I would once again dream of how a classroom should operate: Children would work together cooperatively, interacting with one another about the topics we were studying. They would be independent enough to handle routine problems (the "I don't have a pencil" or "Where is the paper?" category of problems) and be willing to tackle other situations before seeking my help (the "Where do I find that information?" or "How do I start this assignment?" type of problems). I, in turn, would be able to spend a good part of my teaching time watching my students—engaged in a variety of activities, interacting with individuals or small groups—and learning about how they think and solve problems and about what their needs are.

But the reality that ruled me for too many years was quite different. I'd present a lesson to the class, giving information, leading discussion, asking questions. When the time came for students to work independently, I'd give and explain an assignment. Invariably, only seconds after the students began to work, several hands would go up. Some children needed reassurance, others further directions or a different explanation, still others just wanted some additional contact from me in order to get started. By the time I had reexplained to these students, several others needed attention. Soon I was being pulled from student to student, responding to request after request, often with the same information.

Finally I had enough. I reorganized the basic structure of the classroom so that, using the same content and curriculum materials I've always valued, I could move closer to my dream and farther away from the reality I had lived with for so long. This classroom management scheme is called "groups of four." It's a system of cooperative learning that requires reorganizing the classroom physically, redefining the students' responsibilities, and carefully structuring my role as teacher.

Reorganizing the classroom

The physical reorganization first. Just as the name implies, the class is organized into groups, with four students seated together in each. Arranging the students into groups of four is easy enough. If you're lucky to have tables, you simply seat four at a table. If not, you can move the children's desks into clusters of four. Since one of my goals is to have students work with everyone in the class over the course of the year, I assign groups randomly and change them regularly (see "Questions Teachers Ask" on pages 60 and 61 for more about this). The system I use to assign groups involves a deck of playing cards. I label each table or cluster of desks with the number of a playing card (ace, two, three, and so on). I then select out the corresponding cards and shuffle and distribute them. All the children who hold aces go to the ace table, all those who hold twos go to the table labeled two, and so forth. I like the randomness of this system. It takes the responsibility off my shoulders, especially in elementary classrooms where boys often feel it's an unfair fate to have to talk to girls, or where cliques of kids like to work together to the exclusion of others. Neither of those two situations is acceptable to me, and the cards provide a good way around them.

Three necessary rules

Three rules are in operation when students are in groups of four:

1. You are responsible for your own work and behavior.

2. You must be willing to help any group member who asks.

3. You may ask for help from the teacher only when everyone in your group has the same question.

I've found that these rules need to be explained and discussed for at least the first half-dozen times I put students into groups.

The first rule is not new for any student. Even so, it helps to clarify it with further explanation: You have responsibilities in this class, and your job is to meet them. If you don't understand something, what you need to do first is to ask your group for help. On the other hand, if you do understand, don't take over and give answers; listening to others' ideas is one of your responsibilities. Sometimes, even though you are sitting with your group, you will have an individual assignment to complete. Other times, your group will have an assignment to complete jointly, and then your responsibility is to contribute to the group effort.

I often clarify *the second rule* about helping members with two comments: Notice that the benefit of this rule is that you have three willing helpers close by at all times, with no waiting for help. Also, remember that you are to give help *only when asked*. I caution students not to be pushy, to wait for group members to ask, and to help, not merely by giving answers, but by trying to find questions that will help someone focus on the problem at hand.

The third rule—to ask for the teacher's help only when everyone in the group has the same question—is pure gold. It eliminates most procedural concerns such as "What are we supposed to do?" and "Can we take this assignment home?" And it directs students to seek help from one another first, relieving me of having to give the same directions or information over and over again. I know that when I'm talking to the entire class, it's rare to have everyone listening attentively. Groups of four help enormously. I figure that at least one out of every four students is listening to me at any one time, and I take my chances that one has landed at each table.

Staying true to this rule was extremely difficult for me at first. It's usual during initial groups-of-four experiences for individual children to come to me with a question or request. When that occurs I ask the child if she's checked with her group, reminding her that when I see four hands raised, I'll come and discuss whatever problem there is with the entire group. At first, responding in this way was contrary to my vision of myself as a responsive, sensitive, helpful teacher. No more; I'm now firmly convinced that requiring children to rely on themselves and on one another is invaluable in helping them become confident and independent. In addition, when students are asked to take care of their own needs, they have more opportunity to voice their thinking and respond to others' ideas.

Getting started

There's part of me that wonders how I survived before this groups-of-four period in my teaching. The system has become that ingrained. I don't mean to suggest that seating students in groups of four and explaining their responsibilities will produce instant success. Although students have heard about cooperation, working together cooperatively is not a skill they've necessarily had practice with. And although

they have always been told that they're responsible for their own work and behavior, meeting that responsibility independently doesn't seem to come naturally. It takes a great deal of practice, encouragement, and discussion for students to learn to work together successfully. For me, learning to respond to students in groups of four rather than to individuals required time and attention and the breaking of long-standing habits in teaching behavior.

Best beginnings

I've found that the best beginnings come from problem-solving situations that challenge students, pique their curiosity, require them to come to a group decision, and call for a group record of their results. It's helpful to find problems where the students can see and realize the advantage of pooling their thoughts. And it's important to find problems that all students can grasp sufficiently to make a contribution to the group.

One good starting problem is an arithmetic activity. It calls for each group to find all the ways to write the numbers from 1 to 25 as the sum of consecutive numbers. I first explain what *consecutive* means, and then I model for the children what they are to do. I use 9 as an example because it is the sum of more than one set of consecutive numbers ($9 = 4 + 5$ and $9 = 2 + 3 + 4$). I tell them that some numbers won't work, and challenge them to see if they can find a pattern for those numbers. They are to search for other patterns as well, and to write summary statements describing the patterns they find. (For younger children, finding the consecutive sums for the numbers from 1 to 15 may be sufficient. For children who work quickly or for gifted children, the task can be

extended to include higher numbers.)

I do not tell the children how to approach sharing the work. I do not tell them how to record, other than providing them with suitable paper and requiring them to put their group label (ace, two, three, etc.) as well as each group member's name on their recording sheets. How they work and how they record the results of their work is up to them. I also have groups post their results when all the groups have finished. That way, groups can compare their results and how they organized the recording.

I've found that in tackling the consecutive sums problem, some groups divide up the numbers so that one person does 1 to 6, another does 7 to 12, and so on. Other groups just work on whatever numbers each individual wants and add their findings to a group chart. Some groups have one person do all the recording; others share that job among the members. All of these differences are important to discuss so that students become aware of the variety of ways to make decisions and solve problems. And it's from these discussions that I get valuable insights into my students' approaches to learning and to each other.

Their recording systems differ as well. Some groups list the numbers from 1 to 25 and write the sums next to each. Others organize the numbers by how many different sums they found for each, recording all those that could be written in only one way in one column, those that could be written in two ways in another, and so on.

Sometimes a group will summon me to ask if they should orient the paper the long way or the short way. I tell them it's up to them to decide. Often what seems a minor decision to me is a major one for children. Organizing themselves on paper is a skill children need to acquire; the group recording decisions help them acquire it.

The teacher's role

When you launch the students into an activity, you need to be sure that they understand the directions clearly. It may also be helpful to review the rules for group work. Once the groups get started, your job is to circulate without drawing attention to yourself, to observe the interaction, and to help when an entire group has a question. While circulating, listen to the groups' approaches, ideas, and methods; this information will be useful when summarizing with the class later.

If groups are working well, avoid intruding. When a group has bogged down, however, you need to intervene. Your goal is to get the group working productively and independently, so you need to determine the nature of the problem, offer assistance, and move on once the group gets going.

Two types of problems occur, each calling for a different type of intervention. One problem is difficulty with the activity itself. The group is either stuck or is pursuing an incorrect line of thought. If they're stuck, you need to help them restate what they know so far and suggest another way for them to approach the activity. If they're pursuing an erroneous idea, you need to point out the inconsistency in their thinking. Optimally, you do this by asking a question that forces them to face their incorrect reasoning, not by telling them what their error is.

For example, a group of students working on the consecutive sums problem found that 2 and 4 were impossible to write as the sums of consecutives; then they decided that all even numbers would be impossible. "What about $1 + 2 + 3$?" I asked them. When they realized that the sum of those numbers was 6, they had to reevaluate their hasty generalization. Once the group understands the inconsistency, leave them to rethink the problem.

But the difficulty may be not with the activity but with the group. For a group to operate successfully, four roles are usually present: the doer, the questioner, the prober, and the summarizer. When one of these roles isn't being carried out, the group process bogs down. For instance, if there's no doer, the group may lack the impetus needed to get started. This condition may be obvious because students don't have the necessary materials—paper, pencil, blocks, whatever. Someone has to get them started, and that person is the doer. The questioner helps to focus the group on the task at hand, perhaps by asking: "What are we supposed to do?" or "Didn't she say to do it this way?" The prober makes comments or asks questions that go further, that get at the meat of the problem, such as: "Is there a pattern here?" or "How can we tell if we've found all the ways?" or "There's probably a simple way to look at this." The summarizer is the one who notices and gives feedback about what people are doing; it's a supportive role. During group work, none of these four roles is fixed to individuals; they'll often shift from one student to another.

Keep these descriptions in mind as you circulate and listen to groups working. When a group isn't functioning, your job is to join the group (bringing up a chair or kneeling to get at their level), provide the missing role, and leave when they're on their way independently. For example, if the group is supposed to produce a joint recording, as in the consecutive sums problem, and if after circulating through the class I notice that a group doesn't have the paper for their record, I'll join that group. "How are you supposed to record your results?" I'll ask, playing the questioner. This way I find out if they understood my instructions about which paper to use. "Who will get the paper for your group?" I'll then ask, prompting someone to take on the role of doer. As soon as that responsibility is assumed by a group member, I'll leave the group.

Sometimes a group has written all the sums they can find and calls me over to announce they've finished. However, when I look at their recording, I notice that they haven't written any summary statements. The usual response is that they can't think of any. So I'll ask some probing questions to get their thinking kindled:

QUESTIONS TEACHERS ASK

What's so special about four in a group? There's nothing sacred about putting four students together in a group, but there are reasons that make it a convenient and useful size for a group. There are enough children to provide for a diversity of ideas, yet not too many to hamper individual participation. The even number allows for partner activities within the group, without the problem of an odd person being left out. A group of four isn't a mandatory aspect of this organizational scheme, but it seems to work well.

What happens if the class doesn't have the right number of students to make groups of four? It's rare that a class has an exact multiple of four students. In the majority of cases, you'll have to have one group of three, five, or six students to make up for the discrepancy.

How do you group the students? I do it randomly, with the playing card system described in the main article. This is important to me, since I want my students to be flexible and comfortable enough to work with any of their classmates. Sometimes students ask to sit in groups of their own choice, and once in a while I let them. Then we discuss the results of that grouping procedure. And once in a while, for a specific task, I'll choose to group certain students together. If I do so, I like to be open with the class about my reasons.

What if one student doesn't want to sit with another? I don't allow that option. I explain to the students that it is important to me that they have the opportunity to benefit from all of their classmates' thinking, so they'll be expected to work with whomever draws the same cards. It's true that some groups work better together than others, but it's very rare that a group finds it absolutely impossible to work together. If that does occur, my advice is to treat it very seriously and openly with your class.

How long do you keep students in the same group? It varies, but my goal is to have students in the same groups for a week or two at a stretch. I find that students need time to learn how to function well in the groups, and for this reason, I'll purposely structure one or two experiences a week specifically to practice the rules of organization. These experiences may range from half an hour for younger children to an hour or more for older students. I also think it's a good idea to establish a routine for changing groups. There are times when children love their groups, and would prefer not to change. There are other times when they can't wait to be free from a particular group. If you set up a pattern of giving out new cards on Mondays, for example, you'll have one less issue to cope with during the year.

"Can you see a pattern to the numbers that are impossible? How could you describe that in a summary statement? What do you notice about all the numbers that had three possible sums? Or four possible sums? Which numbers had only one possible sum?" When I see that they've begun to consider some of my questions, I walk away, allowing the children to respond on their own. Or I may help them word a summary statement if I feel they need more support.

When groups have finished exploring a problem, it is your responsibility to summarize the results for the entire class. Post the recording sheets so that everyone can see them, and ask the class to look at differences and

---

If the groups are working well together, is it all right to leave them together for a longer period of time, even for half the year or more? How often to change groups is a decision you need to make based on your own situation. But the flip side of letting groups stay together because they're working well is that you'll change groups that are not as successful. I think that might give the message to the students that they really don't have to iron out their own problems, that you'll rescue them if the going gets a bit rough. Since my goal is to have children benefit from *all* of their classmates' points of view and to learn to succeed in a variety of situations, I'd rather change them more often, even if the groups are working well together.

Is it desirable to have leaders in the groups, either chosen by the students or by the teacher? Leadership occurs in the groups in a variety of ways. The child who gets the materials organized assumes leadership in one way. The child who asks probing questions for the purpose of clarifying performs the role of focusing the group, acting as leader in yet another way. At times, I'll ask each group to appoint a spokesperson to report to the entire class about the group's opinion or results; that person may be seen as a leader for that purpose. It doesn't make sense in this setting to have a fixed leader. I'm interested in nurturing cooperation in the groups; I don't feel that establishing a hierarchy of power supports that.

What about the student who won't participate or cooperate or do the work? This situation isn't one caused by the groups-of-four organization. The problem with that student would exist anyway in your class. Perhaps the problem is more noticeable to other students in the grouping arrangement, since students are more aware of what others are doing. You'll have to deal with that student in the way you always have.

What about the noise level? There's no doubt that talking makes a room noisier. Students may need to be reminded if the din gets unbearable, but you have to remember that their talking indicates their active involvement, and that is an important aspect of learning. I've found that the noise becomes less of a problem with time. Maybe I have just gotten used to it, but it's not an issue. There is still quiet time during the week in the class, and I still can get all of the students' attention when I need to.

similarities in the organizational methods of recording. Review the summary statements, being sure that when incorrect generalizations appear, you provide counter-examples for the students to reconcile. Ask groups to report how they divided up the work. Ask them if they felt their method was a good one, and if not, how they would change it if they had to extend this task to include the numbers from 25 to 50. Discuss both content and process issues during the summation.

This discussion period is most important. It's the time when groups report on their conclusions and discuss differences. It's the time when you set right faulty generalizations and take students' ideas further. Remember, you're not giving up your teaching role in the groups-of-four situation; you're heightening individuals' involvement in the exploration part of the learning process, and helping them to understand the results of that exploration.

Benefits to learning

Organizing a class into groups of four does more than provide a useful management technique. It provides for a learning environment that serves children's intellectual development. As explained by Piaget, interaction is one of the essential ingredients for learning. What the grouping does is maximize the interaction that occurs among students.

A key element in group explorations is that students get to exchange their thoughts about various subjects with each other. In these discussions, they justify their viewpoints, validate facts, deal with contradictions and, at times, alter their attitudes. From becoming aware of different points of view, children are encouraged to rethink their own ideas and approach objectivity in their understanding. This is when learning occurs. It requires a classroom setting that is safe enough for children

to risk trying out their ideas, one where the emphasis isn't always on being right, but on exploring ideas.

The groups-of-four system provides a way to implement a curriculum where not only is there room for errors, but where errors are seen in light of their potential for new understandings. It provides a structure for student interaction where the answer is not always the main goal, and where the emphasis of the classroom is on children's active learning, not on the teacher's presentation of information.

Just as there is no substitute for firsthand experience in learning for students, there is no substitute for your learning about the potential of this grouping system by trying it yourself. Even if it is for only one period per week, give yourself the opportunity to use this method as a way to help your students develop independent learning skills and foster problem solving in your classroom. If you can switch classes with another teacher at your grade level for a short period of time, then try an activity twice, once with your class and once with another. That will give you double the benefit in terms of your own experience.

Activities do not have to be specially created for groups-of-four work; they can be adapted from those curriculum experiences you regularly provide for your students. The following suggestions are ones friends and I have tried and found successful in the classroom.

● *Language Arts:* Each group is to draw a five-by-five grid large enough so that a word will fit into each box. (Draw one on the board as a model.) Brainstorm with the children five categories for which they'll find words that belong. Some suggestions to get them going are foods, animals, things you find at school, colors, and so on. Write these categories on the left side of the grid, one for each row. Then choose five letters and write one at the top of each column. Children are to find words for each category that begin with each of the letters. Older students should try to find words that they think will be different from other groups' so that a point will be earned for each word that is unique. For younger children, perhaps one category is enough, with the children finding pictures from magazines to cut and paste in the boxes.

● *Science:* To explore the concepts of time and hypothesis testing, groups generate a list of activities they do that generally take about 3 minutes. Some examples are: brushing your teeth, putting on your shoes and socks, getting your books from your locker, and so on. Then they devise a way to test each action. Compare groups' results.

● *Mathematics:* Provide each group with small cardboard squares (about 1″ or 2 cm on a side) so that each group member has five squares. They'll also need paper ruled into a grid with spaces the same size as the squares. The group is to find all the ways to arrange five squares, following the rule that edges must always be completely touching.

This is OK:

This is not OK:

They should cut each shape they find out of the grid paper. They should check all their shapes to make sure that they really are different. If one can be flipped or rotated to match another, then those two count as the same figure. When the group is satisfied that they've found all the shapes they can, they tape their shapes on a sheet of paper and post them.

● *Social Studies:* Have groups decide what would be the ten best items to put in a time capsule that will be opened in 100 years by students the same age as they are now. Ask them to rank the items in order of importance. Compare groups' lists when they're all complete.

Marilyn Burns is the creator of *The Math Solution* in-service courses, now taught nationwide. She is the author of nine children's books, including *The I Hate Mathematics! Book* and *The Book of Think.* Her latest book for teachers is *A Collection of Math Lessons.*

Break the ice with Five Squares

Five Squares is a simple, nonverbal, uncomplicated game that, like so many of our simplest activities, has a way of making magical things happen. It works well with all age groups—try it sometime at a department or faculty meeting—but it's more fun with kids because they're more open. If you use it with early elementary kids, the follow-up discussion might not be as intensive as described here.

Five Squares creates experiences and events that enable students to observe themselves and others in a group. The depth of these observations tends to be curtailed more by the teacher's inhibitions than by any limitations the students might have. At the very least, the game has a socializing value. As a first-day "mixer," it brings kids together in tight little groups and fuses a sense of cooperation among them. By gently coercing youngsters to join a group, you are helping them overcome both the awkwardness of those first days and the inertia that makes it so hard to meet new people. You can bring into the class those few kids who always sit on the periphery, somehow excluded or excluding themselves from the action. Because it is a nonverbal game, Five Squares is fun even for those students who don't speak English very well or, for that matter, don't speak it at all.

Five Squares is an experience in observing human behavior close up. As the groups go about their tasks, many kinds of behavior appear—anxiety, frustration, impatience, conflict, hostility, cooperation, indifference, interaction, isolation, withdrawal, and aggression. Discussing these things is only inciden-

tally an outcome of the game; more important is the understanding gained of what happens when individuals become part of a group.

Making Five Squares

Five-Squares sets, even for huge groups, can be easily and cheaply made from materials available in school. Paper squares will last five or ten classes; cardboard will survive an entire department. Squares may be of any size, but I find that pieces cut from 6- or 8-inch squares fit into 5- by 8-inch envelopes. The following directions are for one Five-Squares set:

1. Cut out five paper or cardboard squares, all the same size.

2. Cut each square into segments, copying the five patterns from the diagrams in this article. (You should have a total of 15 pieces.)

3. Sort the pieces into five envelopes (three pieces per envelope; see page 74 for suggested groupings), making sure that no envelope contains a perfect square.

Playing the game

OK, the bell has rung. It's 8:45. Let's come down off the walls. Pull your desks together into groups of five... that's right, so that they form a little table. (Pandemonium; desks scraping across the floor; books, pencils, and gym shoes everywhere; loud talking, kids bumping and stumbling into each other—the usual comfortable, familiar classroom sounds.) Not too close, let's keep the groups apart so you can't see what people in the other groups are doing. George, you look awfully lonely over there by yourself. Why don't you join a group?

Do I have to?

There's a group of four over there that needs you.

Naw, I'm staying here; they don't need *me*.

Let's see...one, two, three...we have four groups of five, a group of four, and George. We're going to play a game today called Five Squares, a really simple game that you play with pieces of cardboard. But to play, you have to be absolutely quiet. No one can talk or make a sound while the game is going on. Now, I've put the rules on the board and we'll read them over together to make sure everybody understands. Once the game's started, you can't talk and I can't answer questions. See, I have to

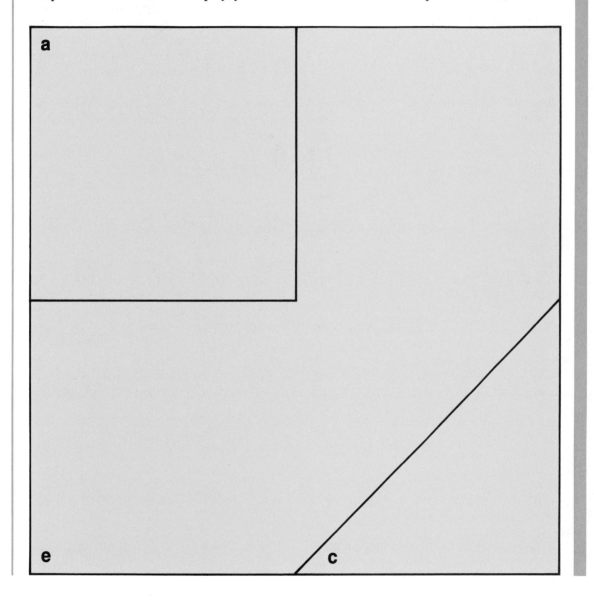

be quiet too! First, here's what you have to do:

[GROUP TASK]

To complete five squares in such a way that each player has a square the same size as the other players.

In other words, everybody's got to end up with the same size square.

[RULES]

The game must be played in complete silence. No talking.

You may not *point or signal other players with your hands in any way.*

You may not *take a piece from another player.*

You may not *place a piece in another player's square.*

You may *give a piece to another player.*

When you have finished, cover your square with your envelope.

It's a giving game. Now, you'll each get an envelope containing three pieces, but don't open it until I say to. This is a group task and you will be competing with other groups against the clock. Any questions?

My group didn't get any envelopes.

Hmmmm. Well, only groups of five can play this game, Leona, so I guess you're out—unless you can convince George over there to join you. All right, remember, no talking and no fair taking pieces from another player. Just give. It's 9 o'clock; open your envelopes and begin. You will have 40 minutes to build your squares.

(Students open and go through their envelopes, inspect each piece, and begin looking around at the other players. At first they try to make squares from their own pieces, but it quickly becomes clear that they will need pieces from other players. How to get them is the problem. The group of four looks completely forlorn; they're glancing at George, who

sits alone, aware of their glances, looking very self-conscious and uncomfortable. Pieces are moving around the tables. It is a struggle at first to keep everybody quiet. With uncharacteristic sternness, I caution Robert and Bill against taking pieces from each other. Moving from group to group, I make my presence felt, increasing the anxiety and frustration somewhat, and enjoying close up the squirming, furtive glances and contortions that bodies are put through in attempts at nonverbal communication.

At 9:07, group 3 finishes. Players cover their squares and look around and realize that they are the first to finish. Their faces reflect triumph. Leona comes over from the group of four and whispers...)

We're bored just sitting over there. We want to play, too. Can't you make George sit with us so we can play?

Why don't you go over and talk to him about it? Take him out into the hall and see what you can do. (Leona goes over and nudges George, who reluctantly follows her out into the hall.) Those of you who have completed your squares can get up and observe the others—quietly—if you like.

(At 9:15, group 1 finishes. They get up and watch the agonies of the two remaining groups with smug satisfaction. Group 12 is at an impasse. Loretta has a square that looks like this:

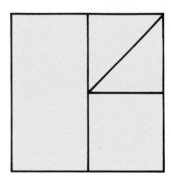

and she has pieces belonging to two other play-ers. She has covered her pieces, indicating that *she* is finished with the game, and is beginning to look bored with the others. She leaves her group, walks around a few minutes looking at the other players, and then comes over to me.)

Can I go to my locker? I have to get some-thing.

Don't you think the group might need you, Loretta?

No. I'm finished, and besides, they're so slow. They just sit there.

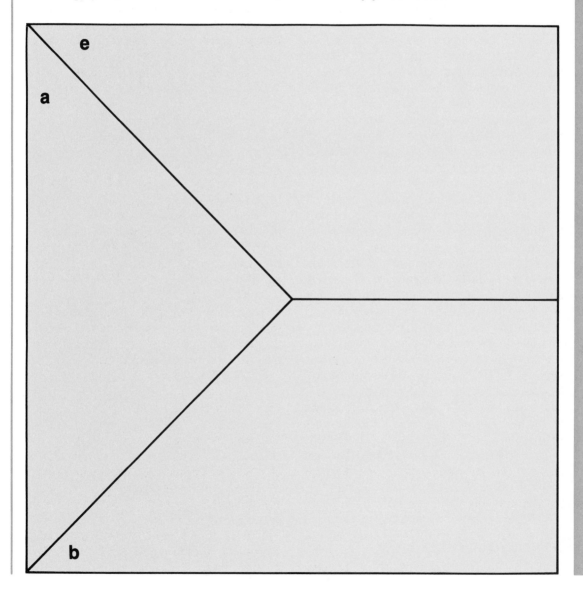

(Loretta leaves the room. Her place is now empty; her pieces, incorrectly arranged, are covered. It is now 9:20 and two groups are still working. George and Leona have returned. George has moved his chair over and sits with the group—still defiant but considerably more cooperative. I have given them envelopes and they are playing. The game continues with the three groups—2, 4, and 5—still working. There is a lot of animated gesturing, signs of impatience with fellow players. Frustrations are high in group 2. Loretta's departure has left them helpless; she has still not returned and her group has all but given up. Three members of group 4 have correct squares; the other two are shooting pieces back and forth, trying them out, and then exchanging them again.

At 9:30, group 4 finishes with sighs of relief and released anxiety and tension. They are now the third group to finish and join the others watching group 5. They seem happy to have finished, their humor and animated interaction contrasting with the dejection of the largely unwatched group 2, one member of which has now taken out a magazine and has begun reading. Great activity in George's group 5 now. The late-starters are working furiously and, for his part, George looks contented and amused. At 9:36, they finish. George is bragging about bringing the thing to a successful end; he had the "Y" square which, for some reason, seems to be the most difficult to visualize and usually the last to be completed. Loretta returns and sits down; her group has disintegrated. At 9:40, time is up and the game is over. The members of group 2 look stunned; they are the only group not to finish.)

Time for discussion

That was fun!...Hey, how come Loretta left?...I don't see what that has to do with social studies...We didn't get a chance to finish...How come we did that?...Man, that was really too simple....

It's supposed to be simple, Barry. Remember I said that it was a nonverbal game, a simple game? Well, because it was so simple, we had a chance to concentrate on the other things that were happening. But before we say too much about what the game is supposed to be, let's find out about how it actually worked. What do you think this game was about, Larry?

Well, it was a cooperation game. You know, because you couldn't talk to one another, you had to really work together to get things done.

Mike?

Like you said, it was a giving game. I sat there for like 10 minutes waiting for someone to give me a piece, and then it hit me: everybody else is doing the same thing, waiting for everyone else to give. Then I started moving my pieces around, hoping—well, as sort of a signal to the others...

Ann?

You've got to think like the other person's thinking; you know, you've got to think what they're thinking so you can know which piece they need and look to see if you've got it.

George?

I think it was just fun doing it. I mean, once I got into it I wasn't thinking much about it. I was enjoying playing the game.

Great. Now have you ever heard of the word *microcosm?* A microcosm is a model or a kind of situation in miniature that, because it is so small, is easier to observe and talk about. Do you think these groups of five had anything to do with that sort of thing? George?

Yeah, well, our groups were kind of a small world—like there were all kinds of people in it.

What kind of people, George?

Well, you know, people with all kinds of attitudes and feelings—like people who give and people who take, and helpful people, and people who didn't help, and people who cheat...

Mario: There are cooperative people and uncooperative people...

Ann: Yeah, like Loretta. She just got up and left.

Bill, and Catherine, and the others in group 2, how do you feel about what happened in

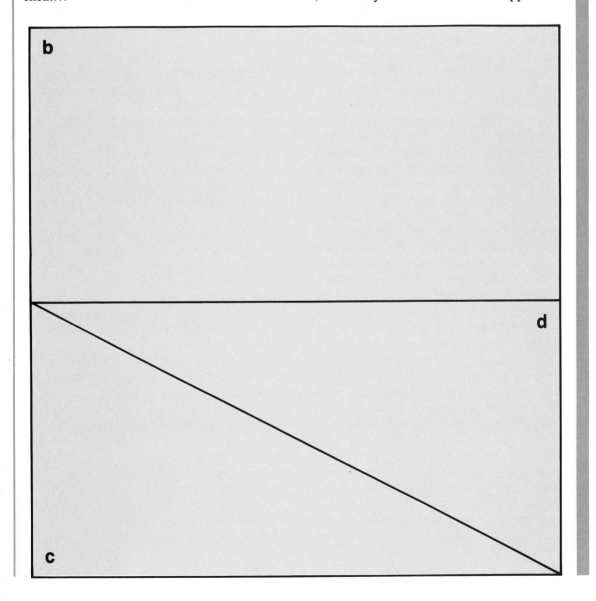

your group today? How do you feel about Loretta? (I'm sitting with Loretta now, to attract and at the same time help her absorb some of the barbs coming her way. I think she feels better about it that way. I want her to face the consequences of her actions rather than just be defensive and ignore the others.)

Oh, I don't know.

Come on, Bill, what were you thinking when Loretta got up and left and you were unable to finish? How'd that make you feel?

I guess I was angry. I guess... She had no right to do that! We could have finished if she hadn't left. Hey, how come we couldn't finish with Loretta gone?

Because the game is designed so that although there are many ways of making squares, there is only one way to do it so that you have all five squares the same size. Loretta's square had pieces in it that belonged to two other squares.

Yeah, we needed you, Loretta, and you took yourself right out of the room.

Well, I didn't know, and anyway, you're all so slow. I didn't see any need to just sit around.

Loretta, didn't you feel any responsibility to the group? Didn't it occur to you, as it did to Mike, that other people were depending on you?

Well... What's the group to me anyway? They don't mean anything to me; they're just a bunch of people playing a game.

(At this, the class explodes. Loretta is not as callous as she sounds, but she is very independent and proud to a fault. Because she has a lot of initiative and an indomitable inner strength, she feels she needs no one and thus cannot understand how anyone could possibly need her. After the initial reaction, the class becomes conciliatory, and Barry, who hasn't said much all morning, begins to see something.)

That's really scary. Loretta isn't the only one, you know. When I was playing the game, I was just thinking about myself. At first I tried real hard to make a square before anybody else did. I bet that if I had gotten my square I would have done the same thing. A lot of you would have, too; you just won't admit it. That's really terrible. We're all like that.

(We continue to explore the conflict between the individual and the group, and some students begin to talk about how they think their self-centeredness and competitiveness are somehow part of their upbringing. Many feel that working together hasn't been stressed enough in school and in our society.)

George: I think we need practice. You know, it sounds strange and all that, but I don't think we know how to work together.

Then you think it's a good idea that I ask you to work in small groups a lot rather than working as individuals all the time?

Yeah, the group is better, with more of us working together on a problem.

But did you get more out of the group experience than just completing a task? After all, it wasn't a very important task. Loretta?

I feel like I know some people better in the class now. Like you, Raul. I never talked to you and now that we have been sitting together I feel like I know you better.

George, what did you get out of the game? You really didn't want to play, did you?

It was all right. It was fun once I got into it.

Leona: Why didn't you make him play with us from the start? You're the teacher; you should have told him to get himself over here and play with us.

How about that, George? Should I have done that?

Well, sometimes, you know, it just takes

time. Sometimes you just have to ease into it. I'm careful, man, I just don't jump into everything. I may like it, and I may not. It's hard to tell.

How did you feel about Leona talking with you about playing?

I didn't think it was none of her business what I did.

But you listened to what she had to say and decided to play.

Leona: I still think that as the teacher you should have insisted that he play. That's what

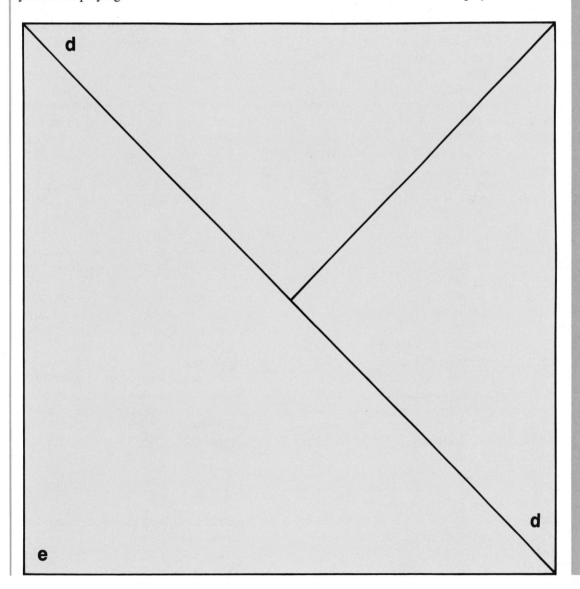

I would have done.

But, Leona, I respect George's right not to play. And I respect him for listening to you and, when he did decide to join the group, really chipping in and helping. I don't do everything I'm asked to do. There are lots of situations that make me feel uncomfortable and threatened. What would really be great is if we could talk about those things, like we are now, so that everybody understands how we feel.

(The class is really together now. The reticence is gone; we've become very comfortable with one another. We're laughing a lot, caring a lot for others. I ask Leona and George to role-play the alternative situation in which Leona, as teacher, confronts George directly with his refusal to play. He becomes hostile and defiant in his role, forcing Leona to admit that even though my way isn't right, neither is hers. We're high on interaction, talking in a way we never have before. Greg, another student who keeps to himself, speaks up today.)

I liked the game.

Can you tell us more about what you liked, Greg?

I don't know; it was just good. I felt like other people were trying to help me. I mean, I was the last one to finish and I really felt like everybody was pulling for me, you know, giving me the right pieces and moving around to show me what to do. I had the right pieces, but I just couldn't get them to fit. Finally, Bill moved a piece so that I could see how it went.

Why do you think he did that? It was against the rules.

I think he likes me. I think he wanted to help me.

(Later we talk about how it felt to be last, or not to have finished at all. Students who are used to success in school and in life generally failed at the task, while others known as "failures" or "problems" were in the first group to complete their squares. I direct a question to a very bright student who was last in her group to complete a square and, in fact, had to be helped. This is one of the few times in her life a simple task has eluded her. It is important to me, particularly in a class of such diverse abilities and interests, to get this into the open.)

Geraldine, you didn't do too well. How come?

I just couldn't get it together. It looked simple, but somehow I'm just not used to that kind of problem.

How did you feel—not in an intellectual way, but from inside?

Everybody was looking at me, waiting for me to finish. They were so impatient, like I was dumb or something. I was angry with myself, and I hated all of them for being so smart. I kept saying to myself: "It really doesn't matter; it's just a silly old game anyway."

Does that give you any insights into how others in the class must feel when they can't answer a question or do an assignment, can't "get the pieces together"?

Yes, I can understand. I think it must be painful to be last all the time. It must hurt inside to not know and not be able to do what everybody else seems to be able to do so easily. That would hurt a lot. I think I would want to help someone like that.

A bond is made

Other questions come up during the morning, and we discuss them:

How did you feel upon first joining the group? How did you feel later?

Did you cooperate with the others from the very beginning?

At what point did your attitude change?

Was your first thought, "I'm going to be the first one to complete a square"?

What were your feelings when you heard we were going to play a game?

How did you overcome not being able to talk? Did you use your eyes more, your hands, or what?

How do you feel about communicating with people nonverbally? Did it bring you closer in

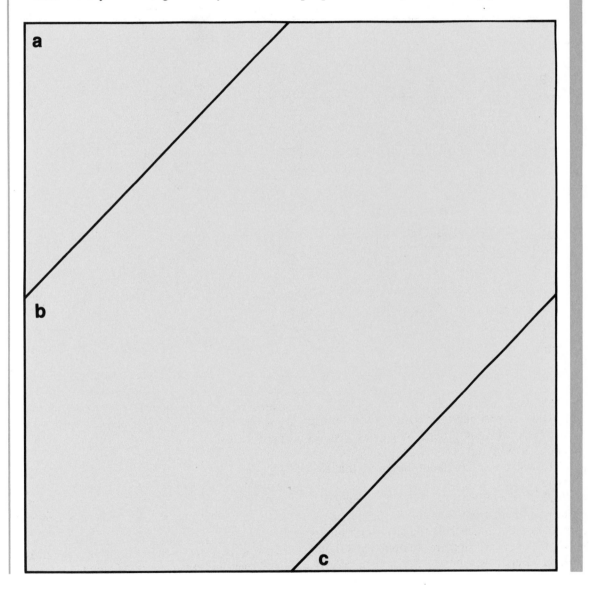

Five-Squares Groupings

Here's how to sort the pieces into the envelopes so no child gets a perfect square. Each piece is keyed by letter to the forms illustrated.

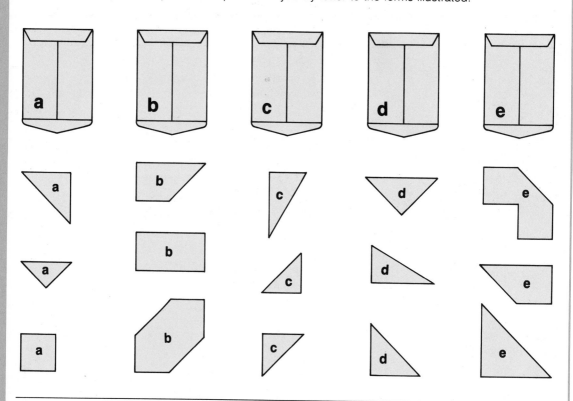

some ways? Did it isolate you?

Did you feel angry or hostile toward other members of your group? What did you do about it? Why?

How did you feel about the group that finished first?

How is working in a group to complete a task different from working alone?

When the lunch bell rings, no one jumps for the door. We sit there wishing that it didn't have to end, looking at one another. Slowly, everybody gets up and leaves for the cafeteria, not wanting to break the bond that has grown between us.

David Weitzman is a free-lance writer, photographer, and illustrator of numerous books on historical subjects, curriculum development, and museum educational programs. A former teacher in elementary through university levels, he is an adviser and consultant to numerous historical, cultural, and educational committees and projects in California.

Games for more than the fun of it

As the school year begins and plans are being made for a revitalized reading (math, science, etc.) program, it might be worthwhile to take a new look at games—an area that has far more influence and potential than most of us realize.

Games are important. They can provide opportunities for building a sense of community and trust within the classroom. As well as being great "ice breakers" at the start of the school year—how to deal with all those unfamiliar names and faces—they can help develop an ongoing feeling of support and caring among the class.

Young children joyfully "play games" inside and out—with energy, laughter, and seriousness too. Through games, children discover much about themselves, their environment, and other people. They learn about sharing and taking turns, about supporting one another and cooperating with the group. They learn to think quickly, to follow rules, and to observe limits. And they become involved in the group process.

Unfortunately, games are often used thoughtlessly. Insensitive use of games can be harmful to the group as a whole as well as individually. Elimination games, for example, are really only "fun" for the fast, well-coordinated players. The slow or awkward person who is always out on the first round is likely to develop an animosity toward *all* games. Competitive games tend to create barriers between people by setting up a situation in which the players work *against* each other. Noncompetitive, "no win" games, on the other hand, can help create the kind of environment in which everyone can work and play together, where winning or losing is no longer the criterion of success or failure.

Responsible game selection involves both a concern for feelings and a desire to provide for enjoyable group-building recreation. As we consider the potential players and their needs, we try to avoid games that leave people out, that force children to participate unequally. At the same time, we can be searching out, collecting, and even creating games that focus on establishing rapport and good group spirit. The game descriptions that follow provide some examples of game activities in the cooperative mode. (You'll notice that in these games we have consciously and consistently avoided calling anyone "it." The word "it" is a depersonalized pronoun that carries a lot of negative connotations. We refer instead to "the center person," "the leader," etc.)

Name games

When a group is meeting for the first time, such as at the start of a new school year, an active name game can help develop a positive atmosphere and ease the tension of being with new people. It's good for children to realize that people can help each other remember names, and that there is nothing wrong with not knowing everyone's name right away.

Animal Name. Circle, sitting. In this simple, low-risk activity, children tell their names in turn, at the same time telling an animal they'd like to be. To fix an impression, they may tell something about their animal or choose an animal whose name begins with the same letter: "I'm Gina, and I'd like to be a giraffe so tall I could see all the way to the river."

Jack-in-the-Box. Circle, sitting. The lead-off

person, Cynthia for example, first finds out the names of the four people to her immediate left. She then stands and says, "I'm Cynthia," and introduces the four people on her left (starting with the farthest person): "This is Joe, Susan, Pam, Bob." As each name is said, that person stands up and sits down quickly, creating a jack-in-the-box effect. Then the person on Cynthia's right stands up and says, "I'm Pat, and this is Susan, Pam, Bob, and Cynthia," dropping the name of the person who was previously at far left (in this case, Joe). Again, as each name is mentioned, that person stands and sits quickly. By the time introductions get around the circle, the names will be more familiar and the smiles a little bigger.

Gesture. Circle, standing. This game is physically active and a lot of fun. The person initiating the game needs to encourage spontaneity and keep the pace lively and quick. Each person in turn, without thinking, makes a gesture while saying his or her name. Name and gesture go together in some sort of rhythm. For example, while Bob Jacobs is saying "Bob," he raises his hand. On "Jacobs," he stamps one foot with the first syllable and the other foot with the second syllable. The group together repeats the name and the gestures twice. A visual, nonverbal impression goes along with each name to aid the memory.

Games that encourage laughter

Older children seem less likely to act on natural impulses to touch or reach out to others. They've come to think it's "silly," or it means you're "in love" with somebody, or something like that. Inhibition, embarrassment, fear of being ridiculed become barriers to caring about and supporting one another. A good way to break down this kind of tension is to set up situations where people can take part in humorous, nonthreatening activities together. The laughter will frequently create a more open and friendly atmosphere, which then frees people to be more aware of others.

Elbow/Nose. Circle. (Good for small groups.) The leader, Rita, turns to the person on her right and says, "This is my *elbow*," while pointing to her *nose*. This person responds, "This is my nose," while pointing to his or her own elbow. This person then becomes the leader, turning to the person on the right and naming one body part while pointing to another—to which the response is the exact opposite. Pace needs to be maintained at a lively level.

Elephant or Palm Tree. Circle, with one person in the center. The center person points to someone and says either "elephant" or "palm tree." To make an elephant, the person pointed to bends at the waist, clasps hands, and swings arms like an elephant's trunk. The people on each side stretch both arms over the "trunk" person, imitating an elephant ear. (All three of these gestures must happen at the *same time*.)

To make a palm tree, the person pointed to stands tall with hands clasped together and straight up above his or her head. Persons on each side make fronds by holding up their outside arms away from the middle person and pointing them away from their bodies.

If someone makes a mistake or hesitates a fraction too long, then the center person of the threesome moves to the center of the circle. It's a very funny, successful game. People don't mind making mistakes, because everyone is laughing so much. With very small children, it may be better to teach the elephant gesture first and let students practice it for several weeks before introducing the palm tree gesture. Later you may want to suggest other variations or have students make up their own. Examples:

- *Gorilla*. Middle person makes a gorilla face and grunts and swings arms; two side people scratch the sides of middle person.
- *1776*. Center person holds an imaginary flag. Person to right drums a make-believe drum; person on left plays a flute.

(Note: In large groups, have several people in the center.)

Barnyard. Large circle, everyone standing. Choose six animals (fewer for a group smaller than 20) and count off by animals, or pass out slips of paper with the name of an animal on it to each person. Then, with eyes closed, all "animals" of the same kid (sheep, cats) try to find one another by constantly making the appropriate animal sounds (baa-a-a, me-ow). Strategy: When two of the same animals come across each other, they should hold hands and search for others of their kind until they are all together. Remind students that the idea is *not* to finish first, but merely to find their own kind.

One-Word Story. Circle. Each person in turn says one word to add to the story that is de-veloping. For instance, "I... saw... a... monster... in... the... lemon... soup..." and so forth. Again, for best results, keep up a lively pace.

Games that encourage cooperation

When games are being played, it's important to establish a nonthreatening atmosphere. When children have a hard time remembering something in a game, give them some space and allow others to help them. If someone gets

frustrated with being the center person, put in a new center person. The sense of security is strengthened by games in which everyone must work together so that the group as a whole may win.

Musical Laps. This is a cooperative version of Musical Chairs. The whole group forms a circle, all facing in one direction, with hands on the waist of the person ahead. When the music starts, everyone begins to walk forward. When the music stops, everyone sits down in the lap of the person in back of him or her. If the whole group succeeds in sitting in laps without anyone falling on the floor, the *group* wins. If people fall down, *gravity* wins.

Human Pretzel. Two people leave the room. Everyone else holds hands in a circle and twists themselves over and under and through one another without dropping hands. The two people return and are challenged to untangle the group. The "pretzel" cooperates as the untanglers try to figure out who goes where.

Knots (a variation of Human Pretzel). All players close their eyes and move around, searching for hands to take. When each person is holding two other hands, the leader has all players open their eyes and try to untangle themselves without dropping hands. The group must work together to get out of the knots. Sometimes the group will end up in one big circle, but most of the time there will be a knot or two in the circle. Sometimes there will be two or more circles, either intertwined or separate. It's great fun and leads to group cooperation.

Attention-out activities

Attention-out activities are light, quick games that help change the focus of attention from preoccupation or daydreaming to what's happening in the room here and now. They serve to clear the mind of fogginess.

B is for Bonnie. Everyone sings the song "My Bonnie Lies Over the Ocean," and whenever a word that begins with "b" is sung, people stand if sitting, or sit if standing:

> *My bonnie* (stand) *lies over the ocean*
> *My bonnie* (sit) *lies over the sea*
> *My bonnie* (stand) *lies over the ocean*
> *Oh, bring* (sit) *back* (stand) *my bonnie* (sit) *to me.*
> *Bring* (stand) *back* (sit)
> *Bring* (stand) *back* (sit)
> *Oh, bring* (stand) *back* (sit) *my bonnie* (stand) *to me, to me.*
> *Bring* (sit) *back* (stand)
> *Bring* (sit) *back* (stand)
> *Oh, bring* (sit) *back* (stand) *my bonnie* (sit) *to me.*

Variation: Every other person stands up before the song begins. Then, as everyone sings, the standing people will start the sequence by sitting, and the sitting people will start by standing. The jack-in-the-box effect and confusion will add to the fun.

One-Minute Activity I. One person stands up, shakes hands with four other people while singing "Yankee Doodle," and sits down again in a different chair.

One-Minute Activity II. One person stands up, touches her (his) left foot with her right hand, touches her right hip with her left hand, howls like a wolf, and sits down again.

Try thinking up a variety of one-minute attention-out activities. Or ask one child to be in charge of thinking one up and leading the group.

Inventing your own games

Most of our lives are spent looking to others for ideas and instruction. We are so used to following others or going to a book to get ideas that it is hard to feel confident in our ability to create something new, to try something untried. Children in particular are wont to look to parents or teachers for direction. But the fact is that all of us, children and adults, are capable of innovating, if given the opportunity.

Game inventing is an activity that both develops innovation skills and leads to new games to play and to pass on to others. One way to invent a game is to start with a small group, throwing out ideas, discarding, changing, adapting—until something comes up that is fun to play. As a group, you'll want to keep in mind the particular objectives you hope to fulfill—developing and maintaining an at-mosphere of acceptance, providing for maximum participation and fun—but you'll also want to stay open to whatever may just come up. Game inventing benefits from both structure and spontaneity.

Once you've settled on an idea and tried it a few times, share it with another group and see whether it works for them. You may surprise yourselves, and there's bound to be some fun involved when you're serious about inventing games.

Marta Harrison was a member of the Nonviolence and Children Program, part of the Philadelphia Yearly Meeting, the local organization of the Religious Society of Friends (Quakers). "Games for More than the Fun of It" was excerpted from the organization's publication *For the Fun of It! Selected Cooperative Games for Children and Adults, which is printed within the Manual on Nonviolence and Children.*

Helping students to be more responsible

If you'd like your students to become more cooperative and responsible, the first step is to involve parents—teaching responsibility works best when it's a joint home/school effort.

To encourage parent involvement, send home the letter shown on page 82 (or use the ideas to write a letter of your own). Working with your home/school association, you might also hold a round-table discussion with parents, sharing ideas and strategies on the best ways to encourage responsibility.

What to do at school

Here are some guidelines for nurturing responsibility in the classroom:

Make duty a privilege. Young children love to do real, adult work, especially if they think it's a treat. For example, one teacher made responsibility special by pinning red felt stars on two "duty children" each day. The two students helped her clean paintbrushes, wipe tables, pass out supplies, collect papers, and so on. She also asked the children to look out for others who needed help. As a result, students became more aware of each other's needs and grew closer as a group.

Have more jobs for more people. What are the jobs you normally assign to students? Do they include interesting, challenging tasks as well as duller, more routine ones? To be sure that all jobs rotate to everyone, make a job wheel. You can align students' names with new duties each day or week.

Build autonomy into classroom jobs. Most children relish jobs that require real skill and care. With patience and plenty of initial supervision, you can teach students at any grade level to correctly use such adult tools as a stapler, a three-hole punch, a microscope, a film projector, a computer, and so on. Stress the importance of handling these tools and equipment correctly. Then teach your students how to use them properly and have confidence they'll do it right. Appoint student "experts" who can teach others and help when someone's having trouble.

More pointers

Some teachers let only responsible children take on responsible jobs. I think that's a mistake. Most children are capable of mature behavior, if given the chance. For example, in Beechwood Elementary School (outside of Montreal) the motto is "If you can't take responsibility, we'll show you how." Do as teachers there do:

Expect maturity, even in young children. Says one teacher, "I start by telling one child where I'll be and leaving my class for 5 minutes. If the students are busy and happy when I leave, chances are they will just continue what they're doing. If they act up while I'm gone, I tell them they're not responsible enough to be left alone. That really makes an impression on them."

Pair children carefully. When classroom jobs are assigned, Beechwood teachers pair the less competent children with the more competent ones. They also look for strong points in both students to create a feeling of teamwork between partners.

LETTER TO PARENTS

Dear Parent,

This year, I'm making a special effort to help all my students become more responsible—more willing to help, more aware of the needs of others, more able to work on their own. Specifically, I'm working to:
- *give students interesting and challenging jobs,* not just dull and routine ones.
- *give less criticism and direction.* I praise students for doing the best they can—even if it's not perfect.
- *let students know that their work is really needed.* (Studies show that children are more willing to pitch in and cooperate if they know their efforts will help others.)
- *challenge students to grow.* As they become more skilled and capable, I let them take charge of increasingly important tasks.

If you'll work with me to reinforce these points at home, there's a good chance we'll both see positive results.

Ideas to try at home

Talk with your children about the chores they find interesting and fun, and those they find boring and disagreeable. Make a list of jobs they'd like to try and jobs they want to avoid. The results could surprise you. The jobs your children like might be harder and more time-consuming than the ones they hate. Why? Maybe because the jobs are more interesting or challenging, or they involve real adult responsibilities. Children can feel that same pride and self-confidence we get from doing satisfying work.

Now look at the jobs your children hate. Are they ones like picking up dirty clothes, weeding the garden, making the bed, taking out the garbage? These are the jobs many parents assign children, and children dislike them for the same reasons we do: They're boring. I'm not saying children shouldn't do these things—dull jobs are a part of life too. But they can be made more appealing if you:

- Tell your children you need—and appreciate—their help. If they know you're counting on them, chances are they'll take their responsibilities more seriously.
- Work out a rotation system so that each person also gets to do the more interesting tasks.
- Keep in mind that children don't always have time for chores. Make your system flexible enough to work around sports practices, music lessons, and so on. Try to decide if some chores can be done less frequently or even eliminated.
- For younger children, break jobs into smaller steps so they're easier. For example, making a bed can be frustrating for young children. Showing them how to pull the bed out from the wall, make neat corners, and so on will make the job easier and more pleasant.
- Point out positive results. "Bring your laundry down so you'll have clean clothes for tomorrow." "If we all do the housework together on Saturday morning, we'll have time to go swimming in the afternoon."
- Remember to notice and praise your children when they do their jobs, even if they do them only occasionally at first. Appreciation is the best encouragement.

A support system

For your children, being more responsible will mean accomplishing more things on their own. That's great, but they still depend on us. At this time in their lives, we adults need to be a rock of support, listening to them and taking care of them when they need us.

To help your children become more responsible, I'll give them interesting, challenging tasks (along with the dull ones) and support their efforts to accomplish them. I hope you'll do the same.

Sincerely,

Give fewer punishments and more responsibilities. If two Beechwood children have been fighting, they're asked to put their apologies in writing. Each develops a composition that answers the questions: What did I do? How did the other person feel? Students' papers must demonstrate real understanding of the other's point of view.

Aim for self-help solutions. Learning how to learn is more important than just completing assignments. A sixth-grade student reported doing much better once she began helping herself. When she got frustrated with a problem, she used a relaxation technique suggested by her teacher: Take a deep breath; go back to the beginning of the problem; read it again slowly.

A final note

A spirit of caring, fostered in the classroom, needs natural outlets in the world beyond the classroom. To give your students plenty of opportunity to help others, include in your curriculum such activities as community service, tutoring, beautification projects, and holiday charity drives. When children see how their efforts help others, they'll feel real satisfaction themselves.

Helen Fox teaches and writes on educational topics in Amherst, Mass.

4

COPE WITH RECESS, RESTLESSNESS, AND RAINY DAYS

What to do when the weather forces you to keep your "itching and twitching" students indoors? How to make sure their recess exercise and play time is more than just aimless running about? Better still, how to use recess in different and more productive ways? Here are some teacher-tested ideas you can try.

Nine ways to play tag

Even the best game gets stale with use. But you may not need to replace it with something totally different. Maybe all it needs is a new twist. The following games are traditional variations of the game of tag, but each has a different angle. Because they're familiar, these variations are easy to learn. Because they have an underlying similarity, they can be easily substituted one for another. In fact, you'll probably develop your own variations of what's presented here. If you do—great! It means you're putting the emphasis on *fun,* exactly where it belongs.

1
Duck-Duck-Goose

This game works best with 8 to 15 children. The children sit in a circle. One player, IT, walks around the outside of the circle, tapping each player on the head and saying "duck." At his discretion, IT taps someone on the head and says "goose." GOOSE immediately stands up and chases IT around the outside of the circle. If IT gets back to GOOSE's place in the circle without being tagged, GOOSE becomes IT for the next round. If GOOSE tags IT, GOOSE returns to his seat and IT must go another round.

If you want to avoid the possibility of one child remaining IT for a long time, have IT stand in the center of the circle whenever GOOSE wins the chase. IT should remain there until GOOSE tags another player, who then becomes IT. This allows a slower player

to catch his breath and regain his composure before rejoining the game as part of the circle.

2
Two Deep

This game, involving more children in active play, is a more active version of Duck-Duck-Goose. Because players exchange roles frequently, more players can participate actively.

Have all but two players stand in a circle. The players standing outside the circle are designated as a tagger and a runner. The tagger, who must stay outside the circle at all times, chases after the runner, who may enter the circle at will. When the runner does, she must stand in front of someone in the circle, thereby designating that player as the new runner. The old runner then takes the empty place in the circle. If the tagger manages to tag the runner, they exchange roles.

Because this game moves quickly, the children forming the circle should stand at least an arm's length apart, to prevent collisions. Also, to keep the chase from roaming too far away from the circle, you may need to indicate boundaries within which the chase must occur. Once the children understand the strategy of the game, runners will tend to remain close to the circle.

3
Elbow Tag

This game is almost identical to Two Deep. But because it doesn't use a circle, it invites more group participation for confusion and surprise.

Players form side-by-side pairs with the members of each pair facing in opposite directions and linking arms (elbows bent, hands on waist). Allow ample space between each pair to provide room for the chase.

Select one pair, tell the members to separate, then designate one as the tagger and the other as the runner. The runner tries to avoid getting tagged by linking elbows with either member of a pair. When he succeeds, the other member of the pair becomes the runner. If the tagger catches the runner, they exchange roles.

4
Choo-Choo

Active participation increases with Choo-Choo. Groups of three players form trains, one standing behind the other and holding on to the waist of the player in front. The first player or engine in each group is the tagger. Her objective is to tag the last player, or caboose, of any other train. When that happens, the tagger becomes the new caboose for her train and the new front player, or engine, becomes the tagger.

During the game, the engine tries to block other taggers. The player behind the engine contributes by giving directions that help protect the caboose. Naturally, the train must stay intact during the entire game.

5
Catch the Tail

This game is similar to Choo-Choo, but a bit more strenuous. To begin, have players form trains, as in Choo-Choo. Lengths can vary; try starting off with five or six players. Tuck the tail (a strip of cloth or length of yarn) into the collar or pants of the last player of each train. Leave about 2 feet of the tail exposed.

Have all trains face each other like spokes on a wheel, engines toward the center. At your signal, the head or engine of each train tries to catch the other trains' tails. Trains must stay intact throughout the game. Those that have lost their tails may continue playing until all the tails have been caught.

Keep in mind that this is a fast-moving game, and children may have difficulty keeping their trains together. Consequently, you may want to experiment at first with just two small trains. This will allow the children to get a better sense of the game and give you an opportunity to take any necessary safety measures. If any version of the game proves too strenuous, restrict movement in these ways: Have players keep both feet on the floor and move by shuffling; have them take only giant steps; have them take only baby steps.

For variety, use only two very long trains. Or have each train try to catch its own tail. Or have the players in each train do the bunny hop while trying to catch another train's tail.

6
Link Tag

One player is the tagger. The rest are free to run within the boundaries you've designated. Anyone tagged joins hands with the tagger. The tagging pair continues to hold hands while trying to tag someone else. Each tagged player joins hands with the tagging team; only the players with a free hand can tag. The game is over when everyone has been tagged.

If the game is too difficult for the first tagger, move the boundaries in to reduce the chase area. Or begin the game with two taggers, each creating a separate line until one line gets tagged by the other. If children enjoy this version, try beginning the game with three or more taggers.

7
Fishnet

This is a variation of Link Tag, except that it has a two-part objective. First, the tagger, or fisherman, tries to tag four other players. Once he has, the linked team of five fishermen tries to encircle, or net, each of the remaining players (or fish).

Players may try to escape the net by dodging under the fishermen's arms, providing the circle is still open. For variety, have the players keep their arms at their sides while trying to break through the net.

8
Pom Pom Pullaway

Play this game on a rectangular field, about 100 feet long by 15 feet wide. All players except one are asked to line up behind a baseline at one end of the field. The extra player is the tagger, who begins the game by chanting, "Pom pom pullaway. If you don't come, I'll pull you away!"

With that, all the players run toward the opposite end of the field, trying to avoid getting tagged. Any tagged player remains in the field and tries to tag other players. Players are safe only when they make it across the far boundary.

Once the remaining players have made it

across the boundary, the taggers chant in unison, and the runners try to make it back to the opposite boundary without getting tagged. The game continues until no runners remain.

9
Lemonade

This game begins with two teams at opposite ends of a playing field. One team decides on an occupation to pantomime, such as lawyers, garbage collectors, bakers. That team begins the game by marching forward a few steps, all abreast, while saying "Here we come."

The other team takes a few strides forward, saying "Where from?" The first team names their city and takes a few more steps toward the second team. The second team, again marching abreast a few steps toward the first, says "What's your trade?" The first team, marching and chanting, says "Lemonade." The second takes the final few steps, saying "Show us some if you're not afraid!"

The first team then pantomimes its occupation as the second team shouts their guesses. As soon as players in the first team hear the correct guess, they run back to their end of the field, trying to make it across their boundary before getting tagged by members of the other team. Any player tagged by the opposing team becomes a member of that team. The opposing team then prepares the pantomime for the next round. (Note: While one team is preparing a pantomime, the other is usually planning strategies or their next pantomime.)

Bernie DeKoven, a former elementary school teacher, is president of Playworks, Inc., a consulting firm in Palo Alto, Calif., producers of computer-enhanced meeting systems.

TIPS FOR AN ALTERNATIVE RECESS

Some of the alternative forms of physical activity include:

Infinity ball

A variation of volleyball. Ball, net, and two teams as usual, but the teams can be mixed as to age, sex, and physical prowess without anyone risking failure. The object of both teams is to keep the ball in the air, each team hitting the ball three times on its side of the net and on the third hit, sending it across the net in a way that sets up the other team to do the same. If the ball drops, blame is shared equally between the team that missed it and the team that delivered it. When Infinity Ball was played at the New Games Tournament, sponsored by Stewart Brand (the originator of *The Whole Earth Catalogue),* spectators remarked on the cheerfulness and energy of the mixed teams and the absence of grim losers.

Beanbag relay

A way of helping younger children improve their coordination—again, without winners or losers. After two teams have lined up, a person from each runs out. One has a beanbag, which he throws to the member of the other team. They throw it back and forth four times and then run back to their respective teams. The rest go in turn. The goal is simply to complete the exercise; no score is kept. Variation: members from each team hop, jump, or skip out and back, trying to finish at exactly the same time.

Relaxation exercise

Try this in a gym period. Have the pupils lie down with closed eyes. In a soothing voice, ask them to be silent and let a few moments pass so their breathing can become regular. Then ask each student to pay attention to his/her right foot. Ask him to hold the foot tense for 10 seconds, then relax. (It's OK for each student to hold his breath as he tenses, but remind him to breathe as he relaxes.) Ask the students to repeat the process with the left foot. Continue the process all the way up the body, including the eyes, ears, and top of the head. At the end, give students time to enjoy the experience of having their bodies completely relaxed.

Choose a color

This is a standard creative drama exercise, but it can be used just as well in a gym period. Have each child silently choose a color. With eyes closed, have them imagine coming close to the color—in whatever form it takes for them. Then have each child enact the color in free, creative movement. Usually, children see that each child's movement is unique—even when the colors chosen are the same.

Imagination training

Children are asked to perform a task—running down the field or perhaps doing a gymnastic maneuver. Then they are asked to sit or lie quietly, eyes closed, and visualize themselves doing the task perfectly. Then they perform the task again. The results usually are better the second time.

Beyond the merry-go-round

The bell rings for recess. What does that mean? Time for fresh air and exercise in the play yard? Yes. A chance for kids to run around, let loose pent-up energy, yell? Perhaps. A break from learning? Certainly not!

Our play yard, small as it is, is a discovery lab, a truly open classroom, where independent learning occurs all year long. It's a place where children become observers, inquirers, naturalists. It's a place where children learn to perceive and appreciate, in the words of William Blake, the "minute particularities" of nature.

If your play yard lends itself at all to nature study, consider using it this way more often. Nature study is not something to be relegated to a once-a-month "nature walk"; it is an on-going process, a spontaneous interaction between person and environment that happens all the time. Children need to know this. They need to become aware that whole worlds exist right at their toe-tips.

What is the role of the teacher? To be the catalyst. To notice new things every day and to introduce them to the children. To nurture curiosity with infinite patience and to direct inquiry, so that the children answer their own questions. To help the children see connections.

This is not a scientific essay that describes a unit or lesson. It doesn't tell how to do anything. It is merely a scattered recollection of playground nature experiences.

Exploring the plant world

Beyond the merry-go-round, in a six-foot square of ground, four children sprawl on their bellies, peering at British soldiers through magnifying glasses. They are fascinated with the brilliant red of the fruiting tips. We talk about the red coats of real British soldiers. "Is the red part a flower?"

"No, this is a special kind of plant that doesn't produce flowers; it's a *lichen*."

The children enjoy the forms and textures in this miniature world of nonflowering plants. They like to feel the mosses. They ponder the relative sizes of things as they watch ants creep through the green stalks on their way to and from their nests.

We go on a fungus hunt, and soon find delicate black mushrooms hiding in the grass and a few puffballs. We pick a firm puffball and break it open to watch the little worms eating tunnels through the white flesh. Another mature puffball is stomped upon by one of the children, releasing its cloud of spores.

On another day, the higher plants capture our attention. We compare the forms of mustard flowers, cinquefoils, king devils, and dandelions—four different yellow flowers all blooming at the same time. We choose the two that are the most alike. We compare the white flowers of wild strawberries with the yellow cinquefoils. We study the structure of violets and gill-over-the-ground. All of this teaches classification skills and lays the foundation for math skills.

We pick bouquets of goldenrod from bud stage to seed stage. We examine the embryonic seeds in the inflated sac of a blooming bladder campion, and listen to the rattle of a dried seed pod from last year's plant. I warn the children not to pick the strawberry blossoms, lest there be no berries for our resident cottontail to nibble.

We talk about the methods Mother Nature uses to plant her garden: Wind. We blow on dandelions in spring and milkweed in autumn. Animals. We carry burrs on our socks.

Some questions are hard to answer: "Why is there poison ivy?"

I evade the question by countering, "Why is there anything on the earth? Poison ivy is just protecting itself with its poison." (This coming from a person whose eyes swell shut with the rash.) "Let's look at this locust tree. How does it protect itself? And what about these brambles, and these multiflora roses?"

Playground critters

One day, a fine lesson in protective coloration presents itself in the form of a spider. As I am accepting yet another bouquet of goldenrod, a vivid yellow crab spider drops onto my hand. We compare his appearance on the flowers to the appearance of a black jumping spider. "Which spider could hide better from a predator?"

The jumping spider seems doomed, until we examine his strategy for survival. The children giggle as he jumps from one little hand to another, acrobatic leaps of incredible distance, considering his size. "Do you think he has good eyesight?" We look for his eight eyes, and admire his iridescent turquoise mandibles before letting him go.

Other small creatures of the play yard include caterpillars, moths, butterflies; daddy longlegs clinging to the back wall; singing crickets; bees with pollen-laden legs. We hunt for spittlebug nymphs. We expose the secret colonies under rocks and watch the frantic reactions of minute creatures at having the roof ripped off their world. We replace the roof and do a butterfly-life-cycle dance.

Some days are bird days. We watch the garbagemen of the sky, turkey vultures, slowly circling on tilting wings. A red-tailed hawk searches for food. We speculate about what he might find.

Our playground is not without visiting and resident mammals. Though seldom seen, they leave us clues to reveal their presence: fresh soil around the ground hog hole; meandering mole ridges in the grass. I hear cries of "Jan, I found eggs!" The "eggs" are really rabbit droppings.

Winter brings its own inquiry. We track a rabbit in fresh snow. "Here he was hopping along slowly, probably looking for food. But look how far apart his tracks are by the sliding board; he must have been running. Was he scared by a predator? Ah, look—dog tracks over here."

These are but a few of the investigations that take place on our playground, an area that most people consider barren. When possible, I extend the experiences by directing the children to appropriate books, reading related stories, taking poetry dictations, encouraging artistic interpretations. But the direct experience is, I believe, the important part. It need not be connected to any lesson plan or curriculum area. Each experience becomes a part of the conceptual framework being built in the mind of the child.

Give children the freedom to explore the natural world with all their senses. Help them to know the trees not only by their shapes, but by the feel of their bark; to smell the flowers and the damp earth; to taste mint and sassafras tea. Encourage them to become truly familiar with familiar places. For only through familiarity do we love, and only through love do we protect. Our earth needs a generation of loving protectors.

Jan Jones was formerly a teacher at Apple Tree Children's Center, Castleton, Vt.

Hockalloon: A rainy day winner

Hockalloon (from *hockey* plus *balloon*) is a game invented to meet some rather stringent specifications: It had to be at least mildly physically educational, preferably competitive, playable within an absolutely ordinary classroom without requiring extensive setup or cleanup, capable of sustaining interest, and utterly harmless to players and any academic equipment in the vicinity—including the teacher.

Hockalloon fills that bill. Here, in brief, is what happens: An offensive team of five or six players is provided with eight inflated toy balloons. The offenders try to dribble the balloons—upward—the length of the classroom and to hurl or waft as many as possible into contact with a 4-foot-wide section of the chalkboard. Three defenders try to prevent such contact by downing the balloons or batting them out of bounds.

Those are the basics of a sport that has thrived in my junior high classroom for the past 6 years. It began during one of those homeroom activity periods when we owed a few minutes to physical education. But the weather outside was cold and rainy and occasionally sleeting. The alternative was a study hall that the kids didn't really need and I didn't really want to monitor. And there were these balloons, left over from who knew what event, in my desk drawer...

Lots of leeway

Hockalloon, like sandlot baseball, can be played with varying degrees of organization and complexity. Teachers who want to start their own Hockalloon franchise (they're free; have one) may wish to simplify or elaborate on the original version.

The equipment is beautifully plain: You'll need only balloons and masking tape. The balloons must be round and approximately 8 inches in diameter when nearly filled. Although I have the kids play with eight, there is nothing particularly sacred about the number; you may wish to adjust it.

Set up the court by moving the desks to one side of the classroom. One side wall becomes one out-of-bounds area, and the barricade of desks becomes the other. You may use tape to mark a boundary line down the middle of the room, but the tape is really only needed to mark off the horizontal court areas. (See diagram.)

Starting Line

BACKCOURT

SEMI-GOALIE AREA

FORECOURT

Ultimate Offensive Line

NO-CONTACT AREA

GOALIE AREA
Goal

The goal is an area of chalkboard. The top and bottom limits are defined by the top edge of the board and the chalk ledge, respectively. Draw vertical lines on the board to create a goal area 48 inches wide.

Another sort of goal, such as a large piece of cardboard, could be improvised. The chalkboard offers an advantage, however. In a close or tie game, where the correct calling of a goal is crucial, the board can be chalked over. A balloon hitting the goal area will leave an unmistakable, telltale impression in the chalk.

A round of Hockalloon play is similar to an inning of baseball. In the "top half" of the round, one team is on offense, the other on defense; in the "bottom half," the roles are reversed. In Hockalloon, one round is a complete game unless the score is tied. In this case, the game goes into extra rounds until one team comes out on top. (This doesn't happen often. The "world record" for a single game is four rounds.)

Outnumbered defense

Only three team members play on defense: a goalie and two "semi-goalies," the latter so named because they play about halfway between the starting line and the goal. The goalie's job is obvious. The semi-goalies try to prevent a balloon from reaching the forecourt. Unlike offensive players, goalies and semi-goalies are allowed to grab and hold a balloon.

The five- or six-person offense starts in the backcourt with the supply of eight balloons. Any number of the eight balloons can be put into play at once by any number of offensive players. Just as a basketball player must dribble the ball when advancing up or down the court, a Hockalloon player must keep bouncing the balloon in the air, at least 3 inches above the hand. He or she may never simply hold the balloon or allow it to rest on an open palm.

The first offensive task is to get the balloons past the semi-goalies. Most teams place one or two offensive players in the forecourt, without balloons. The other players put the balloons in motion. They try to advance them through the semi-goalie area or to pass them over or through the semi-goalies to their teammates in the forecourt.

The semi-goalies cannot step over the lines of their area. If a pass is errant, or if the balloon simply wafts out of control, a semi-goalie will make the balloon "dead" by batting it out of bounds, or by grabbing it and "downing" it to the floor. Once a balloon is dead, it cannot be used again.

Forward motion

When a balloon has been safely passed into the forecourt, the player in control advances it as far as the "ultimate offensive line." Offensive players are not allowed to step beyond this line, and the goalie is not allowed to step beyond the goalie area, but either may *reach* across the lines. As the diagram indicates, this creates a no man's land between the offensive players and the goalie. This buffer state prevents physical contact, but it's narrow enough that an alert goalie can reach out and bat down the balloon of an unwary offensive player who is bouncing it too near the goalie's reach.

An offensive player may attempt a goal as soon as a balloon has been brought or passed safely into the forecourt. But the offenders may also elect to wait until there are two, three, or more players with balloons in the forecourt, all tantalizingly kept in motion near the ultimate offensive line. This is the prelude to a barrage of balloons directed at the chalkboard at some set signal. This is known as a "goalie's nightmare," and usually results in at least one

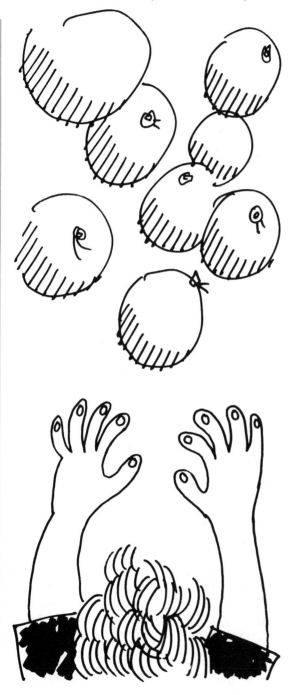

goal. A goal is scored, of course, when a balloon hits the goal area.

If a balloon hits the chalkboard outside the goal area, it is dead, even though it may bounce back. A balloon that has scored a goal is likewise dead, and cannot be used again. If the goalie bats a balloon back without its hitting the floor, and an offensive player takes control of it, it's still live and can be tried again. A goalie obviously tries to bat an oncoming balloon out of bounds, or grab it and down it to the floor. Each half-round ends when all eight balloons are dead. (You may shorten the game by ending half-rounds when fewer than the total number of balloons in play are dead.)

Learning spin-offs

The teacher's job through all of this? Station yourself at a vantage point where you can see the goal area easily and can call the scores. A word of caution: Kids can become very intense over Hockalloon competition; it may be wise to deliver a referees-are-only-human-and-they-may-occasionally-make-mistakes-but-they-have-to-call-'em-like-they-see-'em address at the beginning of the game or season.

If you play Hockalloon on anything like a regular basis, a five-team league, with five or six players to a team, works best. The teams should be as evenly matched as possible, and each should have a proportionate number of boys and girls. The most workable method of achieving this balance goes as follows (this works well, by the way, for any other sort of team choosing):

Put the names of all those who would like to be team captains (usually most of the class) in a hat. Pull out five. These five then retire with a class list to the hallway or an adjacent room. There, following the order in which their names were drawn, they "draft" their teams one player at a time, with the stipulation that there must be X number of boys and girls on each team. The captains return with their lineups. The facts of who was chosen first, last, eagerly or reluctantly are not a matter of public announcement or record.

Choosing a name is each team's first task. You might want to give some guidelines, or even preface the name-choosing with a microunit on alliteration, rhyme, and assonance. Some of our more imaginative kid-chosen names from the past have been: the Interplanetary Planktons, the Maroon Baboons, the Waterful Wondermelons, the Horrible Hemoglobins, and the Intergalactic Tacticians.

A good math activity for the kids is to keep the league statistics. A basic set is simply a won, lost, and percentage record for each team. You might also want to include a "GB" ("games behind" first place, as in baseball). And you can add still others—average number of goals scored and allowed by each team, etc.

Is there any further academic justification for this pleasant diversion within the hallowed halls? Composition? Journalism? You can publish the *Hockalloon Herald* at regular or irregular intervals.

Art? Team emblems and posters.

Creative writing? Team slogans and fight songs.

Oral communication? Kids can tape a commentary on a particularly significant round of Hockalloon action. They can take turns being "anchor person" and "color person."

We've even discussed how/why a team that barely placed third in "Most Powerful Offense" somehow ended up winning the most games—and how this might reflect the "game of life."

Jim Auer teaches eighth-grade language arts at Saint Martin School in Cheviot, Ohio, and is a freelance author of six books and many short stories and articles.

MUSICAL EXERCISES

Here's a simple exercise that combines music and movement to familiarize children with the notes of the scale and to relieve some of the pre-spring restlessness that may be growing in your classroom.

Assign a body part to each syllable of the scale: *do*—toes: *re*—knees; *mi*—fronts of thighs; *fa*—hips; *sol*—waist; *la*—arms (cross in front); *ti*—shoulders; *do*—top of head. Children then follow a leader (you first) who moves up and down the scale—physically as well as vocally—touching toes, knees, etc., while singing the appropriate syllables.

After traveling up and down the scale in this way a few times, the leader may change the tempo. And when children become familiar with each syllable/body part correspondence, the leader may try skipping steps in the scale, developing such musical/movement patterns as do-mi-sol or do-sol-ti-do.

The more adventurous and agile may try performing the syllable-and-movement version of "Twinkle, Twinkle Little Star" or "The Birthday Song." Whatever the melody, minds and bodies will get an enjoyable workout on these twitchy indoor afternoons.

WINDOW WATCHERS

Spring is in the air, and staring out the window is fast becoming the most popular pastime in the school. It is exciting to see the changes spring can bring, so instead of drawing the drapes, shades, or blinds, why not help the class share what they're looking at?

Suggest a few guidelines for sorting out and listing some observations. These suggestions can be written on the chalkboard or appear at some "observation post" learning center. And since the possibilities in "look fors" are endless, the list can be changed often.

Students record observations for listing at random moments during the day—and should, of course, be able to point out any of the observations that are of a concrete nature. And if they're supposed to be looking for "something yellow," "the sun" doesn't qualify if the skies have been cloudy all day.

Here are some look-for starters:

1. What can you see that's hard?

2. What can you see that's red?

3. Look for something beautiful.

4. Look for something that begins with the /b/ sound.

5. Look for something that makes you sad.

6. Look for something taller than you.

7. What can you see that moves? (You'll have to take students' word on this one, since whatever it is may have just moved on.)

8. What can you see that's round?

And for a little vocabulary enrichment:

9. Look for something *stationary.*

10. Look for something that would interest an *arboriculturist.*

The look-fors might involve math, art, creative/critical thinking, as well as other skill areas, depending on the level of the class and what seems appropriate to your current problem.

Some kinds of observing have the potential for developing into discussions, more extensive writings, or science activities. Gazing out the window can be more productive than it appears at first glance.

BEFORE-SCHOOL OPTIONS

Has your collection of before-school ideas petered down to a choice between having students copy the week's spelling words or drill with math facts? Injecting more diversity into the early-morning activities isn't as much of a chore as you might think, and it could make a big difference in the morning mood of everyone concerned.

The relatively uncrowded before-school period is a good time for using the typewriter, the microscope, or other popular equipment. Ongoing projects can be taken a few steps further—building the maze for the gerbil, constructing a model, creating a mural or a map. The special housekeeping tasks can be rotated among early arrivals: watering plants, feeding animals, setting up the listening center.

But for students not involved in these activities, you might provide a daily offbeat alternative or two:

● Have a dictionary scavenger hunt. Post a few dictionary-dependent queries on chart paper. Ask, for example: On what continent does an *aardvark* live? Are you a *native* of Boston? What would you do with a *busby*?

● On the chalkboard, write a coded message for students to decipher.

● Provide hand lenses and have students sketch their thumbprints or make detailed drawings of leaves.

● Draw two lines on the chalkboard. Students can copy the lines on paper and build a design or picture around them.

● Provide copies of a map—a mysterious island or an exotic alien planet. Students "bury" a treasure and write directions for finding it. Then they test their directions on a friend.

● Provide string and ask students to measure their ankles, knees, wrists, and necks in centimeters.

● Provide one or several mystery boxes (sealed) that students can explore by sight, sound, smell. Ask students to record their observations and inferences. At the bell, reveal the contents—and perhaps pass around a treat.

● Provide puzzle sheets, hidden pictures, mazes, word-search matrices.

● Play recordings of popular songs and have students transcribe lyrics for a sing-along book.

Concoct a few more ideas, and before-school time becomes something special.

5
IMPROVING THE CLASSROOM ENVIRONMENT

History and our own experience tell us that teaching and learning can take place virtually anywhere. Still, today's schoolteachers realize that the arrangement of physical space can influence students' behavior significantly and make an important difference to the learning experience. Read on for some teacher-tested ideas for making your classroom a pleasant, well-organized place.

Dressing up the classroom

Children learn more in an interesting, well-designed learning environment, and they feel happier in pleasant, colorful rooms. Creating an interesting and colorful environment is the first step in designing a creative classroom.

Use the ideas in this article to make your room more interesting—to add color, to make new display areas, to solve storage problems imaginatively. Remember to leave some simple, restful spots in the room, however; too many fascinating displays and arrangements can overwhelm children, making it difficult for them to focus on an individual object.

Fabric transformations

The fastest and most dramatic way to change a room is to cover as much of it as you can with fabric. In a few hours with a standard desk stapler, you can change an ordinary, even an ugly room, into a beautiful one.

Look for fabric at discount stores. Burlap is inexpensive, but it fades quickly and looks worn. Felt is the best long-term purchase; it costs more than cottons and polyesters, but it lasts forever and makes a good surface for pinning. A wall covered with felt becomes a giant flannelboard and improves the room's acoustics. Felt comes in 72-inch widths and is reusable.

Muslin is another inexpensive choice, and it can be dyed any color. Irregular bedsheets

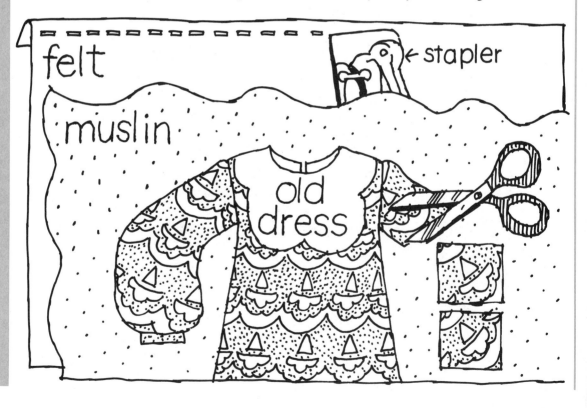

on sale are the best buy per yard, and they can also be dyed. At thrift shops and garage sales, look for plain sheets, curtains, or fabric remnants. Look for large-size dresses too. Some dresses may have enough material to cover a sizable bulletin board or wall. You can also cut the dresses into strips and squares and combine them to make a patchwork bulletin board or small patchwork hangings.

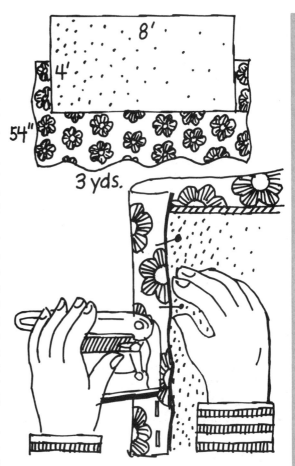

In selecting fabric, choose colors you can live with. Imagine or hold up assorted holiday color combinations against the fabrics. Choose the fabric that looks best with several different colors.

To begin the fabric transformation, cut your fabric 2 to 3 inches longer and wider than the wall space to be covered. Staple the fabric along the top first, turning the edges under as you go and pulling it gently, but firmly, to remove wrinkles. If the fabric is creased, iron it first. Leave perfectionism behind; the purpose of this activity is to brighten the room quickly. In a large room, imperfections won't be noticeable. Don't be afraid to begin; if your work turns out poorly, pull the fabric off and start over.

Look around your classroom for other surfaces that can be improved with bright fabric—cupboards, the backs of freestanding bookshelves, even scratched and battered wood surfaces. Put fabric around the room on tabletops and windows.

Cloth-covered panels

If you have brick or concrete walls in the classroom and can't staple fabric directly onto them, you can cover panels of unpainted soundboard, or acoustic board, with fabric. (Avoid wallboard; it is heavier and too hard for inserting pins or staples.) You'll need 3 yards of 54-inch fabric to cover each 4- by 8-foot board. Cut the fabric 2 inches longer and wider than the board, piecing it if you need to. Place the board on a large table and lay the fabric on it, smoothing away the wrinkles and distributing the cloth evenly. Pin the fabric to the underside of the board, inserting a pin every 5 inches to hold the cloth in place. Then begin to staple the fabric to the back of the board, removing the pins and pulling the fabric firmly, but gently, to remove any wrinkles.

Large sheets of Styrofoam or corrugated cardboard have the advantage of being lightweight; they can be hung from ceilings or nailed or screwed to walls. For an instant art gallery, cover both sides of these Styrofoam or cardboard panels with fabric and hang them in a series of free-hanging rows. (Use pins to fasten fabric to Styrofoam; staples for cardboard.)

Cloth-covered boxes

Boxes can be used for puppet stages, playhouses, play furniture, life-size paper dolls and animals, gameboards, and supply centers. They can also solve most of your storage and space problems.

Purchase boxes at an appliance shop or look in the phone book for cardboard-box manufacturers. Boxes can be ordered in white or brown and in the exact size you want. To get the best price, order in quantity. Boxes of the same size stack and store more easily; 12- and 16-inch cubes are the most practical and versatile.

To staple fabric on a 12-inch box, cut one 13-by-49-inch strip and two 13-inch squares of fabric. Turn one end of the strip under ½ inch. Wrap the strip around the box, pinning the turned end over the other end. Then pin the top and bottom edges of the strip onto the top and bottom of the box, making a fold at each corner so the cloth will lie flat. Staple the fabric in place and remove the pins. Now turn in the edges of the 13-inch squares ½ inch. Pin and staple the squares onto the exposed sides of the box, covering the overhang from the stapled strip. For variety, cut six

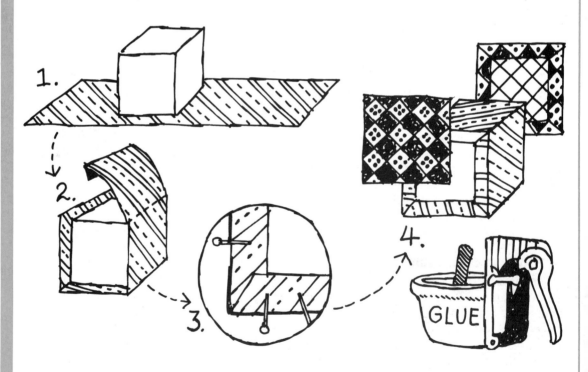

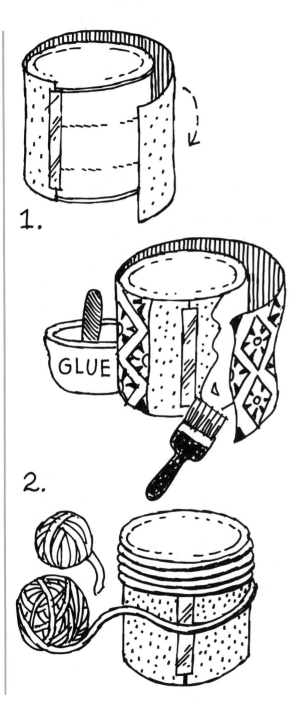

smaller squares in assorted fabrics and staple them to the box using the same method.

It is more work to glue fabric onto boxes, but glue strengthens the boxes, and the fabric is less likely to be pulled off. For this method, mix one part water and one part glue in a bowl. Cut two squares and one long strip of fabric, as you did in the stapling method. Working on a protected surface, brush glue onto the fabric until it is totally covered. Wrap the glued strip around the box, pressing the fabric down and turning the box as you go; leave a ½-inch overhang on both sides. Then press the overhang down onto the top and bottom of the box, making a little tuck in each corner. Turn the edges of the 13-inch squares in ½ inch and glue the squares to the uncovered sides of the box. If the fabric pops up, pin it down until the glue dries. Allow the fabric to dry completely before using the box.

Covering other containers

If you can cover a box with cloth, you can cover a can. Ask a local ice-cream store to save large containers for you, ask the school cafeteria for one-gallon cans, and save your own three-pound coffee cans. To cover a metal can, tape a strip of lightweight cardboard around it and glue the fabric to the cardboard.

You can also draw, paint, or make collages on construction-paper strips, cover the strips with clear Con-Tact paper or laminating film, and tape them onto cans. Putting holiday gifts in cans has become an official enterprise in shopping centers. For pennies, you can make your own gift cans.

Once you begin to look for cans, you'll see that large cottage cheese and yogurt cartons are good storage containers. Even ordinary egg

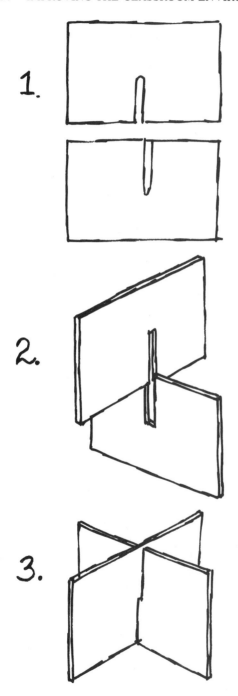

cartons have a variety of storage uses in the classroom. They are terrific for sorting buttons and beads or for individual sewing kits with cups for pins, buttons, needles, and thread. To cover these kinds of cartons, glue fabric onto them or cover them with Con-Tact paper. Then put samples of their contents on the containers; put macaroni on a macaroni container or wrap a can with yarn and put balls of embroidery yarn in it.

Freestanding display units

To form a freestanding display unit with eight display sides, cut two 2-by-3-feet cardboard sheets from a refrigerator box. Then paint the sheets with a base coat of latex paint. Make a slit in the center of each sheet, from the midpoint down, and slide the two sheets together as shown in the illustration. If you want larger sheets of cardboard, for example, 5-by-5 feet, order them from a cardboard-box manufacturer.

Kathryn Shoemaker is an art curriculum specialist for several school districts in California. This article is excerpted from her book *Creative Classroom* (1980). Reprinted by permission of Harper & Row (New York).

Spaces and places for everything

Before the new school year begins, take a few minutes and think—really think—about how and where you are storing your books and supplies. Are frequently needed things located in a convenient place? Are fragile items stored safely? Do students have easy access to books, games, and pictures? Think about your desk. If it always seemed cluttered last year, organize it right now. Make it work for you.

Unclutter your desk

What item now stored in your desk might be placed elsewhere? Perhaps your microscope or that fragile bird's nest should be in the closet. And instead of folding and filing in-

frequently used posters, how about storing them in mailing tubes that can be placed behind books on the bookshelf? (Be sure to label each roll.) Do you need more shelf space? Extend what you have by putting cardboard boxes or plastic cartons (such as milk containers) on top of the shelves. Store materials for different groups in different-colored cartons. Books and workbooks that are used at tables can be stored conveniently in cartons with handles or holes for carrying. Label boxes and bins with simple words that children can read. For younger children, label the boxes with pictures as well as words.

Check the classroom closet

Closet accessory and notions departments in big discount and department stores sell inexpensive plastic and cardboard storage units you might be able to fit in your classroom closet. For example, you could use a small open chest made for storing shoes to store your microscope and other small fragile items such as seashells, seed packages, and models. Other useful storage containers you might find in a closet accessory department are sweater bags, plastic boxes of all sizes, and long, shallow boxes made to fit under beds. You can sometimes buy these things for next to nothing at junk stores or tag sales. Also, parents may have storage equipment they will donate.

Consider hanging storage

What can you hang on the wall or from the ceiling? Look up and around. What kinds of hanging storage systems would make your life easier? You can hang metal mesh kitchen baskets near your desk to store papers, lost and found items, and personal books. Hang another basket, perhaps a straw one, near the door to hold the things you want to remember

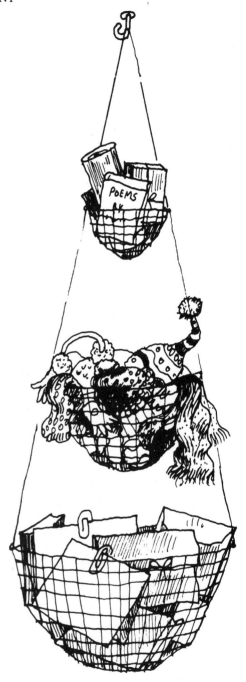

to take home. If plants and terrariums take up too much counter space, put them in special holders and hang them from the ceiling. But before you start screwing hooks into your classroom ceiling, get permission from the school authorities and check carefully to make sure the hooks are strong and will be securely placed. School custodians may have good ideas regarding hooks and hangings and may prefer that you let them do the actual work.

Pegboard is versatile and accessible. Check your hardware store to see the range of pegboard attachments available: hooks, holders, and even little drawers. Large sheets of pegboard can be used to make partitions and room dividers.

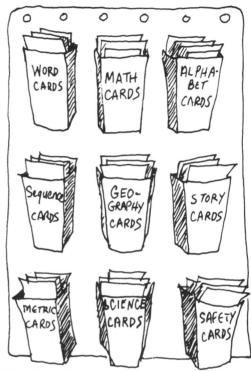

Shoe bags are great for storing activity cards and other small items. Label the outside of each pocket with a wide felt-tipped marker. Make sure the children understand—right from the beginning of the year—that they should return the cards to the correct pockets as soon as they are finished using them.

Hang big rolls of butcher paper or newspaper roll ends from the wall. Ask your custodian how this can be done or check school supply and art supply catalogs for dispensing stands.

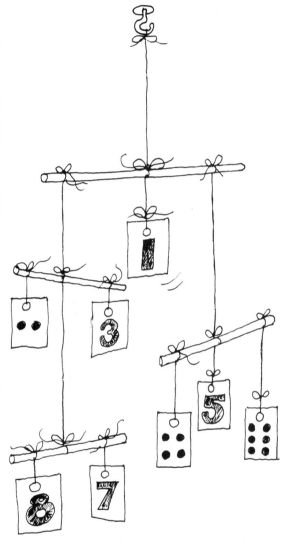

Make one sturdy mobile frame, hang it up, and never take it down. When you want a new mobile, just change the cards. If you make all your sets of cards the same size and weight (using only index cards, for example), you will have to balance the mobile only once. Keep alternate sets of cards in your file drawers. Let the children help you make more sets.

All kinds of storage

What can you put things into? Ask your students to help you collect boxes and plastic bowls for storage. Giant, colorful, plastic-coated paper clips (which are available in most art supply and stationery stores) are useful for grouping different sets of papers. Baking tins can be collected, stacked, and used for individual projects. Ice cube trays are ideal for separating pins, buttons, fasteners, thumbtacks, and paper clips. Toolboxes and fishing lure boxes are perfect for storing manipulative materials such as magnets and geometric shapes. Kitchen cutlery trays are handy for sorting different kinds and colors of pencils, markers, and crayons. An old bureau can be painted and placed in an empty corner of the classroom to hold art supplies. Paint each drawer a different color and, on the front of each drawer, paint the names and pictures of what's inside.

Not enough bulletin board space? Use self-stick cork squares and strips placed singly or grouped together on the wall. You can find these in hardware stores, department stores, and office supply stores. Check with your school authorities for permission to stick the tiles on the wall.

Here's a system for storing homemade games: Buy or make folders with pockets, store the contents of a game in the pockets, label the outside of the folder, and draw a picture of the game near the label. You can keep the folders in a record rack or dish rack in an easily accessible location.

If your school cannot afford to buy fancy storage equipment for your classroom, do not despair. Most of these ideas require little or no money. What's needed is ingenuity and the ability to make do with what you have, what is donated, and what you can get on sale.

Shoe boxes

Plastic tubs or bowls

Old bureaus

Giant paper clips

Baking tins

Ice cube trays

Toolboxes

Kitchen cutlery trays

Self-stick cork squares

Folders with pockets

Record racks

Centers, carts, and catalogs

Learning centers can be located along a wall, especially if there is a lack of space for them elsewhere. Hang a poster and below it attach clipboards, which can be used to hold frequently changed articles and pictures. Then push a table against the wall or, if there's enough room, attach (or ask your custodian to attach) a fold-up shelf at an appropriate height for your students. Things that will be examined at the desk can be put in bags, as shown in the illustration.

If you are a specialist traveling from class to class, you could put your materials in a cart that can be pushed along with you. You might buy a serving cart from the housewares or kitchen section of a department store. If you have to climb up and down stairs, forget the cart. Try a big, roomy shoulder bag and lots of pockets instead.

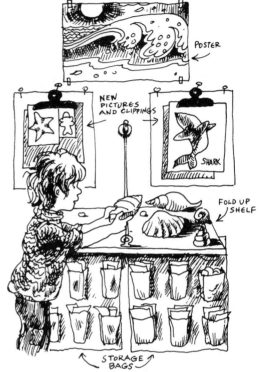

For more ideas about storage, look through catalogs of school supply stores, kitchen equipment stores, department stores, furniture stores, hardware stores, and lumberyards. You'll find ingenious and inexpensive storage systems you might want to purchase or to make yourself. When you buy learning materials, consider ahead of time how they might be stored. Many products have storage systems designed specifically for them.

Jean Marzollo, who wrote "Spaces and Places for Everything," is the author of *Close Your Eyes,* a picture book for children. She is also the editor of *Let's Find Out,* Scholastic's kindergarten magazine. She and **Irene Trivas,** who illustrated this article, have worked together on five books about the education of young children: *Supertot, Learning Through Play, Superkids, Birthday Parties for Children,* and *The New Kindergarten.*

Maintaining things in the classroom

Here are some practical suggestions that can help you keep your classroom environment in good working order.

Opening a new book

To avoid breaking the binding on a brand-new book, keep the book closed and put the back of the book down on a table or desk in front of you. Open the front cover flat on the table. Do the same for the back cover. Then open a few pages from the front and press firmly along the inner margins. Open a few pages from the back of the book and repeat the procedure. Continue doing this, taking a section of pages from the front and then the back, until you have brought the book into the world gently. If your entire class has new books, you may want the students to open their own books, following along as you explain the procedure.

Getting a crayon out of a pencil sharpener

Don't let it happen in the first place! If it does, the sharpener won't work right until all the crayon is out, and there's no easy way to get the crayon out. OK, so it happened. You're going to have to pick and scrape all the crayon off each blade edge. Use an ice pick or a straightened-out paper clip or bobby pin. If it's an electric sharpener, unplug it before you start fiddling.

Maintaining the chalkboard

The custodian probably knows all about special cleaning procedures, but here are a few things you should be aware of: If you're fortunate enough to have a new chalkboard, don't wash it for at least a month. It may be difficult to erase at first, but you can ease that temporary problem by putting chalk on the entire surface of the board (use the side of the chalk) and then rubbing the chalk off with an eraser.

On any board, use only white chalk (medium hard), which is 95 percent calcium carbonate. The bonding agents in colored chalks can leave a coating on the board's surface. Sometimes commercial chalkboard cleaners also build up a coating, which means they probably should be avoided.

Slate boards should not be washed more than semimonthly, and composition boards should be washed no more than monthly. Glass and steel boards can be washed as often as necessary.

Disciplining misbehaving roll-up maps, charts, screens

If you have pull-down/roll-up maps, charts, or screens that are constructed in the same way a window shade is, then you shouldn't have any trouble fixing them. Look at the map (chart, screen, whatever). Is it on a roller with a pin at each end (a flat one and a round one) and are those pins exposed and set in brackets? If yes, you're in business. The flat pin is the important one; it's connected to a hidden-

inside-the-roller spring. The other pin—the round one—is just there to hold up its end of the roller.

What's the problem? The map seems listless? Won't go all the way to the top? OK. Pull the map halfway down, take the flat pin out of its bracket, and then roll up the map by hand. Put it back in its bracket. Repeat the procedure until the map feels right.

If the spring tension is too tight, roll the map all the way up and then take the flat pin out of its bracket and unroll the map by hand. Unroll it about halfway down, put the pin back in the bracket, and repeat the procedure until all works well.

If the map isn't wound too tightly but still refuses to catch and stay where you put it, or if it's forever releasing by itself and racing to the top where it goes bangedy-bang-bang and scares the Beelzebub out of you, then you have to do some investigating inside the roller. Take off the metal cap at the end of the roller where

the flat pin is (remember: the round-pin end doesn't do anything except stay in the bracket). There's a little thingamajig inside there that catches onto a doodad and stops the spring. If the thingamajig isn't broken, clean it and lubricate it with graphite or some other dry lubricant.

The map-screen-chart that wobbles on its way up and down probably has a bent pin (either one) that needs to be straightened out.

The map-screen-chart that binds has its brackets too close together and you can try pounding or bending them a little farther apart. After you've bent them too far, you'll have the problem that's known in the trade as: Falling Out of Its Brackets. This also can be a result of sabotage. Try pounding or bending the brackets closer together.

Operating a movie projector

Go directly to the kid who has a ring of keys dangling from his belt; he's the one who operates the lights for school plays. Ask him to work the projector. If he's out with a cold, ask the girl who fixes up the mikes for school assemblies. If she's out, ask any other kid. As a last resort, operate the projector yourself and keep in mind these things:

Find the threading instructions, which are on the side of the machine, inside the cover, or on a separate piece of paper wadded up under the extension cord. Read the instructions over once and then go back and follow them carefully, *slowly*.

On self-load machines, the leader should be square when you feed it to the machine; otherwise the projector may begin flickering wildly and refuse to accept the film. On hand-threading machines, be sure to make each required loop of generous size; stingy little loops cause vibrating pictures.

Preparing to handle first aid

You may have a school nurse who can handle most injuries (or who can make the best decisions about contacting parents and sending the child for proper medical treatment), but for some injuries or medical emergencies, it is critical that the victim be treated immediately. Treatment can't be covered adequately here, because it requires too many important details. The best advice we can give is that you speak with your school health officials (or write to the sources mentioned at the end of this section) and acquire the necessary information, skills, and equipment that you'll need to handle classroom first aid. Here are the types of things you'll want to know:

What is the first thing you should do if a child in your care has a serious injury or other medical emergency? Who should be called? Who will do the calling or contacting? (For example: If the first person to contact is the school nurse, who will get her? Can one of your students be sent so you can stay with the injured person? Will a nearby teacher have to be contacted first?) When is the school nurse

(or whoever is to be contacted) available? Who should be contacted if the school nurse can't be located? What are the types of injuries or medical emergencies for which some kind of treatment should be given immediately? How do you perform those treatments? What are the kinds of injuries that dictate the victim should *not* be moved?

If you haven't memorized the answers to these kinds of questions, write the answers clearly and concisely and keep them in an easily accessible place. Some information can be handled in printed form (what to do if you suspect a child has ingested a poisonous substance), while other types may have to be acquired in first-aid courses: recognizing and treating shock and severe bleeding; what to do—and not to do—following head injuries; mouth-to-mouth artificial respiration; the Heimlich maneuver for dislodging material that is blocking someone's throat. You may want to keep a first-aid kit in your classroom; the following sources will suggest how that kit should be equipped.

Sources

• The American National Red Cross. Local chapters offer basic first-aid courses and usually have on hand a variety of information resources. These include pamphlets on common first-aid procedures and the *Standard First Aid and Personal Safety* manual, which includes a list of recommended items for a first-aid kit.

• National Safety Council (444 North Michigan Ave., Chicago, IL 60611). The best time to deal with an accident is before it happens. The National Safety Council offers safety education data sheets on a number of topics from "Safety in the Gymnasium" to "Animals in the Classroom." Write for information on obtaining these brochures.

Unsticking desk and cabinet drawers

The easiest way to handle sticking drawers is to rub a candle, bar of soap, or piece of paraffin along the drawer edges and the frame on which the drawer travels. If you're plagued with this problem and want to be fancy and effective, you can make your own lubricating stick. Put half a cup of Vaseline and half a cup of paraffin into the top of a double boiler (never heat it over direct heat). Heat the mixture until you can stir it thoroughly and then allow it to cool until just before it solidifies. Pour the mixture into paper tubes about three-eighths of an inch in diameter and four inches long. (You can make these from ordinary wrapping paper that has been rolled into a tube, taped along its circumference, and taped or stapled closed on one end.) Once the mixture is solidified in the tubes, peel off some paper from the closed end of the tube and apply the mixture to whatever sticks. If this doesn't help, the drawer may need to be sanded; the shiny parts of the drawer's edge indicate where the sticking is occurring.

Be good to your feet

Above all, as they say in the foot business, *wear shoes that fit*. Strange, stylish shoes may look neat, but your feet will be beat. Even leg cramps, bunions, and calluses can be the result of walking problems that, in turn, can be caused by shoes that don't fit.

Shoe sizes are not precise or constant, so rely more on how a shoe feels than on what size it is and what size you think you are. Don't tell the salesperson your shoe size; have him measure your feet while you're standing. (If your feet tend to swell, go shoe shopping in the late afternoon.) Using the measurement as a starting point, continue trying on shoes until you get a pair that is comfortable. If the shoes feel tight, don't expect them to get better after the "breaking in" period. Shoes must feel right, be comfortable, and be big enough when you buy them. If you have one foot that is larger than the other, buy the pair that fits the bigger foot. Proper fit is more important than workmanship. Shop at shoe stores that have the widest selection of shoes so that you have the best chance of finding a pair that fits.

Shoes should have a flexible sole so that the toes can grip at the ground and the foot can bend as you walk. The normal ankle does not need support, and boots and high-top shoes can lead to weakening of the ankles.

And high heels? *Verboten*. While they can make your calves look more attractive by distorting the natural position and action of your foot, they also can lead to ingrown toenails, swollen feet, and bursitis.

The heel of a shoe should align with the heel of the foot and should not jut out behind the heel. Here's why: The best way to walk is with the feet pointing straight ahead, the foot coming down on the back, outer part of the heel and then moving forward to the ball of the foot and pushing off with the big toe. A misaligned heel interferes with proper walking. You can tell if you're walking right by checking out the heels of your shoes; they should be worn off at the back, outer section and not straight across the heel.

If you're lucky, have the right genes, and keep your feet clean and dry, you may never get: corns, which come from friction and pressure and may be caused by bone deformities; calluses, which are protective skin growths that cover areas of repeated friction or pressure; bunions, which are misaligned joints that swell and hurt; warts, which can be mistaken for calluses but which have their own blood and nerve supply and can spread; athlete's foot, which is a fungus skin disease that grows when the skin is weak and wet and warm. And we leave your feet with this thought: All fungus conditions are not athlete's foot.

Controlling noise

Noise is absorbed by things, so if you've moved into a new classroom that is relatively empty and open (or if you've achieved a lifelong dream of cleaning out all the junk from your classroom), you may notice that your classroom is NOISY! The best thing you can do—outside of having carpeting and acoustic ceilings installed—is to bring more *things* into the room. This scientific category of things includes, but is not limited to, fabric screens, beanbag chairs and other soft furniture, inflatable things, stuff on the walls, space definers, book cases full of stuff, stuffed animals, and other junk, stuff, and things.

Controlling classroom pests

Bugs. We're talking about bugs. Major infestations of the school will have to be controlled by pesticides and fumigation, which are not your responsibility, of course. But your class-

room can be the site of minor invasions, and the best overall advice for repelling the invaders is this: Keep your room clean—fastidiously clean. If you're having problems with bugs, pick up all bits of fabric, paper, lint, and food. Any food that must be kept in the classroom should be in tightly closed containers (metal or plastic, if possible) that are kept clean on the outside, too. Here's the lowdown on some specific pests:

Mosquitoes need water to complete their breeding cycle, so if you're having mosquito problems, get rid of all standing water in your room. This includes water in saucers under potted plants. And you may have to pick the larvae out of your fish bowl, because not all fish eat mosquito larvae.

Droppings from classroom pets will attract houseflies, so keep your cages clean.

One of the first places scorpions will head for is the sandbox. If scorpions are in town,

THINGS TO HAVE HANDY IN YOUR CLASSROOM

You'll find it easiest to acquire all this stuff now, early in the year, and to keep it in your classroom so you'll have it when you need it.

- *Screwdrivers.* Two sizes (big and little) of the flat kind and one medium-size Phillips screwdriver.
- *Jar opener.* The rubber disk type works nicely.
- *A first-aid kit.*
- *A guide for removing stains.* A good guide will tell you what equipment and materials you'll need and also will give you step-by-step instructions for removing specific types of stains. (Source: *Removing Stains From Fabrics,* available from Public Documents Distribution Center, Pueblo, CO 81009.)
- *Art gum eraser.*
- *Sewing kit.* Or at least a couple of sizes of needles and two colors (dark and light) of thread.
- *Library scissors.* The kind with the long, long blades.
- *String.* Ball, not pieces.
- *Masking tape.*

- *Jackknife.*
- *Rags.* Lots of them.
- *Hammer.*
- *Laundry marker* (indelible ink).
- *Plastic bags.* Assorted sizes.
- *Ice bag.*
- *Household lubricating oil,* plus graphite or some type of dry lubricant.
- *Tweezers* with a needle nose.
- *Nail clippers.*
- *Change of children's clothes.* Pants, shirt, socks, shoes that seem likely to fit most of your students.
- *Transistor radio.* Nice to have for following big events and vital for weather emergencies.
- *Flashlight.*
- *Jars.* Assorted sizes, with lids.
- *Small wooden* (or sturdy cardboard) *box.* For creatures that are found and captured on the playground.
- *Slippers, heavy socks, smocks,* and any other comfortable or warming or protective clothing that you'll need occasionally.
- *Maps, public transportation routes and schedules,* locations of nearby "landmarks." Get a good street map of the area around the school and mark on it the locations of fire stations, police stations, interesting places such as candle factories and nursing homes, libraries, public buildings.
- *Good, loud, metal whistle.* It can be effective for calling back those kids who've laid siege to an ice-cream truck half a block away from the playground or for letting everyone in the school know that you have an intruder in your classroom. Except for intruder use, blow the whistle only rarely so that it retains its impact and doesn't become a nuisance.
- *Duplicate keys.* To your car, to the classroom, to cabinets or anything else that's kept locked. Do it first thing after the keys are issued to you; do it automatically; don't argue.
- *One good straightedge* with no gouges, marks, or breaks in it.
- *And all the usual stuff:* Scotch tape, paper clips, tissues, staple remover, rubber bands.

encourage school officials to get rid of the sandbox.

Two kinds of spiders that can be dangerous are the black widow and the brown recluse. The widow (female) is about one-half inch long; globular body parts in front and back; shiny black in color; legs long and slender. It may have a red, orange, or brownish-yellow hourglass mark on its underside, but don't count on it. The brown recluse is found in some parts of the south and central U.S.; it's small (three-eighths of an inch) and brown.

Several schools have had infestations of bats. If they come into your classroom, call for help. Do not touch them; they can carry rabies.

Orchestrating your bulletin board and other displays

The cardboard boxes that department stores use to pack shirts or dresses can make for interesting bulletin board frames. Get a few of these unbroken boxes (they're usually an inch or so deep) and mount both the top and bottom on the bulletin board. Then your special material (picture of the day, student story of the week, first flower in spring) can be mounted inside the box top or bottom, which makes a three-dimensional frame for the display. For a varied look, use different sizes of boxes; you also can paste colored paper to the insides of the box tops and bottoms.

Speaking of color, it's usually a good idea that your board and wall displays begin with one basic color and that you keep this color in mind to coordinate two or three (at most) additional, compatible colors on the displays. A lack of a basic, dominant color or the combination of more than three colors can make the display so distracting that messages or learning content becomes overshadowed.

Speaking of overshadowed, that's something you don't want to happen to the messages you mount on the board with cut-out letters, so it's a good idea to make the letters from one common source (note pad pages, for example); to make all the letters the same size; to mount the letters in a straight line. Get fancy with other parts of the bulletin board—not the letters.

Speaking of getting fancy, one way to ensure continued interest in the board is to keep changing it and to link those changes with something that's going on in the classroom: to introduce a new unit; to reinforce concepts and skills taught in the current unit; to display artwork and papers for a recently finished project. A complete change of board for each of these reasons (and others, of course) punctuates the point that the displays or bulletin boards are not just part of the classroom décor but are there to convey messages and learning content to students.

Speaking of students, you might let them decorate the entire room (including bulletin boards) as the year progresses, allowing the room to accumulate a sort of collective personality that is drawn from the projects and papers and pictures that the children choose to display. If you don't like the idea of starting out the year with a nude room, you can put up just enough stuff in the beginning to make the room inviting or you can do the decorating for the first few weeks—until children are comfortable with you, the room, and each other—and then take down your stuff and let them begin putting up theirs.

Picking the right classroom pet

There are good reasons for bringing living things (other than the teacher and students) into the classroom as permanent residents. Young people are naturally drawn to a classroom pet, and when they become partially responsible for the well-being of an animal, they can learn something at least as important as addition, handwriting, or vocabulary.

If the class is to profit from pet keeping, however, the animal must be more than a display. Your task as a teacher is to draw the students' original interest into channels suitable to classroom learning. The following examples of pet programs may suggest ways of involving your students in worthwhile experiences with animals.

Temporary pets and lend-a-pet systems

You may find that you want to test the water before taking the plunge, and in many places that is possible through an animal lending program. Sometimes this kind of program exists within the school. In other areas, small animals, properly caged and accompanied by instructions from the lender, might be available from a junior museum or a nature center.

Typical of good in-school lending programs is the one at the Rocky Hill School library in Knoxville, Tenn. The librarian directs the program, but all students take part as tamers, handlers, cleaners, feeders, and gentlers. The Rocky Hill program provides animals for students to take to their own homes for short periods and always with complete instructions, but it could easily serve classrooms as well.

Many Rocky Hill animals and much of their housing came as donations. Problems have come up from time to time, but there have been surprisingly few difficulties for such an extensive small-animal zoo. And the librarian finds that the zoo complements her reading recommendations. Easter brought in a bunny whose strong personality made *Watership Down* more meaningful.

Parents develop a strong interest in the program, too, and often stop at the library to have a look at "their" mouse (the one they had for a home visit).

Starting and maintaining the class zoo

If you think you're ready to take on a classroom animal but don't have quite enough experience to decide which one to choose, the chart of animals on pages 121 to 123 may be of some help.

The initial cost depends on the animal you choose and the housing it requires. Tropical fish are the most expensive to begin with because of all the equipment that must be purchased. On the other hand, fish, especially live-bearers, are bright and fascinating, and they can be left without feeding or care over school breaks up to 2 weeks long.

The price of the animal itself ranges from perhaps 50 cents for a mouse to as much as $20 for a purebred rabbit or guinea pig. Many of the creatures breed readily, however, and you may find that a student or an acquaintance suddenly has an excess and will donate a beast to your class.

You'll probably have to buy housing. For caged animals the most practical solution is a ready-made cage of the sort your pet store recommends. Makeshift containers may be hard to clean, or animals may find ways to escape from them. Store-bought cages usually have such practical features as slip-out bottoms for easy cleaning, secure closures, and places to keep food and water. For hamsters and mice there are intriguing plastic runs that offer a system of mazes, nests, tunnels, and play areas.

Once you own an animal and its home, you will continue to spend money for food, nest material, and cage litter. As a rule these costs are minimal. A box of grain lasts a mouse or a rat a long time, and you and the students can supplement the grain with whole wheat bread, fruit, and vegetables from unfinished lunches. Some animals require special foods: guinea pigs need greens high in vitamin C every day; birds do better if they have grit; and many reptiles and amphibians require living food. Inexpensive illustrated booklets available in pet stores will give you valuable pointers about care and feeding.

The hidden expense in animal-keeping is time. Animals must be cleaned, fed, and handled frequently and regularly. Students can help while school is in session, but the responsibility is yours during breaks and vacations. Nest material and cage litter must be changed frequently to keep the animal healthy and free of odor, but some animals do part of the work for you. A mouse or rat will turn a lunch bag into finely shredded nest material overnight (and do the same to books and papers if it escapes). Wood shavings, which smell good and are highly absorbent, are the best litter material, but newspaper is an old standby that works.

Warm-blooded creatures need the most care because their rapid metabolisms mean more activity, more feeding, more waste to clean up. Size is another important consideration. Although you may feed and clean a pair of mice only once every week, a rabbit will need daily attention. All animals need fresh water every day.

When beginning or expanding your zoo, you'll have to decide how many animals can be housed in a given space. All the rodents listed on the chart (see pages 121 and 122) under *mammals* will live happily in groups, but if you want members of two species to share quarters, be sure that their sizes and feeding habits are compatible. A guinea pig can be happy with a rabbit, but a mouse and a rat each need privacy. More than two or three mice or rats in a cage may make all the animals nervous. And when dealing with any same-kind group, consult someone who can help distinguish the sexes. Mixing males and females is unlikely to produce a population explosion, but it may well lead to cannibalism or injury to mothers. Also, male mice produce a pungent odor and are not good classroom pets. For breeding purposes, borrow a male mouse from a pet store.

Birds usually are calmer when kept alone, and a single bird can easily be trained to perch on a finger. Several birds caged together may cause too much noise. Parrotlike birds are *noisy*. If you want more than one, obtain and tame them one at a time.

Pet space requirements are flexible, especially if the animals are taken out and handled or released for exercise. Never introduce a new animal, especially of the same species, to a cage containing established residents. Too often family and territorial instincts lead to killings. For fish, the rule is one gallon of water per fish, but you can cheat a little with a filtering system, artificial aeration, and some aquarium plants.

You must also consider what you'll do in case of sickness or injury. It is expensive and may be fruitless to take a sick rat or damaged bird to a veterinarian. An animal may pull through without help if you isolate it in clean, quiet, warm surroundings, but a seriously sick or wounded creature may have to be destroyed. Under usual circumstances, the need to destroy an animal will occur rarely, but if it does happen, you should call a veterinarian and ask for guidelines for using chloroform.

Vacation periods are difficult for teachers who have plans that cannot include animals. Often students solve the problem by taking animals home for the duration or by adopting them permanently, but plan ahead by contacting parents early in the year and asking for a signed permission slip from those who are willing to help out. It is wise to have backup volunteers in case the first choice suddenly decides to go to Aunt Margaret's in Boise for the summer.

An animal in the classroom will give your students a great deal of pleasure and many practical benefits, but just as importantly, *you* may receive a great deal of personal satisfaction from having a classroom pet. There's a certain thrill when you find that a rat is unquestionably pleased to see you in the morning.

ACCENT ON ANIMALS

Animals bring out the best in many children; kindliness seems to come naturally when animals are involved. You might encourage this sort of benevolence—which can often transfer to the human domain—by setting up a program to provide a continuing focus on animals—and kindness—throughout the school year.

Plan about ten projects—with various curriculum tie-ins—through which students can learn about animals and become involved in animal welfare activities. You might contact the SPCA or the Humane Society for information about areas in which public involvement is possible. Set a time limit and a point value for each project.

Among the projects students might choose from:

—Watch a nature documentary on TV. Make note of important facts or major issues to report on to the class.

—Write a letter to a government official on a wildlife or animal welfare issue under legislative consideration.

—Prepare an informational flyer about an animal welfare issue.

—Create a poster to publicize Be Kind to Animals Week.

—Research an endangered species and report on findings.

You might also provide for personalized projects. Perhaps during the year someone will adopt a pet from an animal shelter. This kind of action could be the impetus for a number of tasks, such as keeping records of growth or feeding data, preparing a photo essay about the new pet, or keeping a pet behavior journal.

Action in response to an animal in distress might also be included as a project; however, be cautious that well-meaning but uninformed intervention doesn't cause harm to the res-

cuer or the animal. Discuss problems in dealing with various animal emergency situations and establish guidelines for a response.

Students can become eligible for a special award when they have accumulated a designated number of points. (You might look into renting a popular animal-focus videotape, for example, and offer an "afternoon at the Bijou"—complete with popcorn—when the whole class has achieved award status.)

To maintain a continuous awareness of animals and animal welfare, have students bring in clippings, broadcast or publish animal news they've collected, and update animal-related measures under consideration at various levels of government. By focusing on sensitivity to the needs of living things, you may even note a welcome change in students' attitudes toward each other.

Choosing the right animal

MAMMALS

Mice* (See ratings, page 123.)
Good points: small and generally friendly; many colors; active (give them a wheel, something to climb); eat many kinds of food.
Bad points: males may smell terrible (but are otherwise hard to distinguish from females); too fragile for young or nervous children; partially nocturnal.

Rats***
Good points: very friendly and affectionate when handled frequently and gently; many colors; active; eat most foods.
Bad points: adults often find them repulsive; prone to respiratory difficulties, tumors; may scatter contents of cage.

Hamsters*
(Golden, Teddy Bear, and several other varieties)

Good points: very calm if handled frequently and gently; little cage odor.
Bad points: startled hamsters bite; may be mainly nocturnal, sleepy during school hours; escape and disappear easily; catch human viruses.

Gerbils*
Good points: very beautiful; little odor.
Bad points: may bite; may sleep during the day; may be too active for young children to hold; against the law in some states.

Squirrels (Tree and Ground)
Not recommended for the classroom.

Guinea Pigs**
Good points: very calm when handled gently; no odor; many colors and several kinds of fur.
Bad points: large and need frequent cleaning; catch human viruses; need fresh green food high in vitamin C daily; very nervous if infrequently or carelessly handled.

Rabbits*
Too large and dirty for most classrooms; can scratch hard if startled.

BIRDS

Softbills*
(Smaller varieties include canaries and other finches.)
Good points: easy to care for; males sing; many colors; no special food problem.
Bad points: hard to handle and to catch if they escape.

Psittacines (Curved Beak Birds)**
(Smaller varieties include parakeets, love birds, small parrots, cockatiels.)
Good points: very active (give them a cage toy for climbing and playing); many beautiful colors; fairly easy to train to a finger; may talk or copy noises.

Bad points: untrained birds bite and fly away; produce ear-splitting whistles if insulted or bothered (they decide when that has happened).

Bantam Chickens**

(Enormous choice of kinds, including a Chinese bird—the Silky—that appears to have fur instead of feathers)

Good points: a single Bantam hen is calm and affectionate; may be allowed to walk free inside (outside, too, if she knows you well); extraordinary range of colors; will lay several eggs a week during some seasons.

Bad points: need space or regular exercise; may scratch litter out of cage. Roosters can attack and cause serious wounds with the spurs on their legs; not all males do it, but hens are safer.

REPTILES AND AMPHIBIANS

Lizards (Native)*

(Some common lizards are the fence lizard, the bluebelly, the skink, the horned toad.)

Good points: readily available where they live naturally; easy to feed and to house for short periods; clean. The horned toad is especially docile and has an interesting shape.

Bad points: not available in urban areas (except occasionally from shops); require live food; may escape if carelessly handled or caged; should be released after a few weeks of study. Avoid larger lizards such as the alligator lizard. They bite hard.

Lizards (Exotic) and Crocodilians

Not recommended for the classroom. They are often tropical, require special conditions, may bite, are frequently too large, and may not be released if trouble occurs.

Snakes (Native)**

(Some common native kinds: garter snakes; bull, or gopher, snakes; king and milk snakes)

Good points: easy to house; fairly easy to handle; opportunity to teach the truth about a

creature that excites prejudice; often beautifully marked. Snakes eat infrequently. A temporary captive may be held in a cage with clean water for two or three weeks and then released in the proper surroundings.
Bad points: must have living food of proper sort—frogs, mice, and so on—for each species; garter snakes stink when startled; all may bite if hurt or surprised; may refuse food or have trouble shedding in captivity.

Snakes (Exotic)
Pet stores sell boa constrictors and sometimes other exotics (any snake not from your region). If troubles begin, these cannot be released. Not recommended.

Turtles and Tortoises
These are poor classroom pets. Turtle water spawns bacteria that may be somewhat dangerous. Tortoises, which are expensive, may be mistreated by those who handle and sell them and, therefore, may die after a short period.

Amphibians**
Frogs, toads, newts, and salamanders make interesting short-term exhibits. They need not swim, but must be kept moist because they breathe through the skin. Not good long-term pets.

FISH

Cold-Water Fish*
(Of these, the goldfish is the best. Captured native fish rarely do well.)
Good points: goldfish come in many colors and shapes; easy to feed and to house; easy to find.
Bad points: somewhat lethargic.

Warm-Water Fish*
(Hundreds of species are available. For the classroom, the live-bearers are the most interesting—especially guppies [if kept alone], swordtails, and platys.)
Good points: vivid colors; active; easy to feed; relatively easy to house; may produce young (but the babies are tempting snacks for the big ones).
Bad points: require a heated and filtered aquarium; initial expense high.

BUGS AND SUCH**
During the proper season, a caterpillar is interesting. Collect him with the material he is eating and replace the food frequently. The caterpillar will then pupate and change to the winged stage. Also, try snails, grasshoppers, large beetles, and nonvenomous spiders as short-term exhibits.

RATING SYSTEM
   *** Excellent classroom pet
   ** Good classroom pet
   * Fair classroom pet
(none) Not recommended

Will Kirkman was a freelance writer at original publication of this article.

Creating a classroom exploratorium

What's a museum? Does the word evoke memories of an impressive (and somewhat oppressive) place—all marble and granite? Do you recall displays of valuables in fingerprint-smudged glass cases? Were the halls filled with field-trip children trooping dutifully by exhibits, marking checklists of things they were supposed to be seeing?

Although this stereotype, like most others, has certain bases in truth, try to put aside the unappealing image. The contemporary museum is actually an exploratorium—a place that excites the mind and senses, a place that stimulates inquiry and exploration. Invite your class to join you in experiencing such an exploratorium—in your own classroom.

You might start the experience with what appears to be a most un-museum-like device—a big red arrow. Somehow an arrow demands attention: LOOK and SEE this! The "exhibit" it points out needn't be exotic. It can be something that kids pass, obliviously, every day. Tack that big red arrow above the pencil sharpener. Suggest some questions that can be raised about it: How does it work? Where was it made? How old is it? (Be careful to let the children take over at the first opportunity.) What's it made of? What other ways are there to sharpen a pencil? (For starters, there are electric sharpeners, dime-store gadgets that look like a little globe, a penknife.)

That one big arrow can do heavy duty in any classroom. Point it at the classroom clock, at the plumbing or lighting fixtures, at the ceiling tiles. Move kids a step closer to active involvement by asking them to decide where the arrow will go next. The arrow will soon become shorthand for *look, see, wonder, ask, find out more*. That's the purpose of display—which, like the subtle twist of meaning that makes a good joke, may be most effective when it's simplest.

But display is only the surface function of a museum, the culmination of the museum's efforts. The museum staff's real work starts with a compelling interest in some aspect of how we live and work—our arts, our tools, our ties to history, all the daily customs that form our culture.

The next step, then, in creating a classroom exploratorium is involving kids in the behind-the-scenes aspects of a museum's work—collecting and organizing materials. Museum curators collect almost insatiably, piling up representations of what interests them. Then they bring order to the collection by studying, interpreting, classifying, and cataloging it. Next they select items for exhibit. Finally the curators decide how best to teach through display—how to create the most effective presentations for helping museum visitors see, feel, and fully experience meanings.

Guidelines for collecting

What's to be collected for the classroom exploratorium? How? By whom? There are at least three possible approaches: *individual collections* (each kid serves as curator of his own collection), *a collective collection* (each child contributes something related to a general idea), *a rotating collection* (each child contributes in sequence and thus helps to define a collection that may change in meaning as it grows).

Choosing your collecting approach is almost a toss-up decision. Consider:

• **Individual collections** can help students understand the concept of a collection and can be richer than anyone in the class would expect. Kids have a delightful penchant for collecting anything from stamps and coins to matchbooks, bottle caps, and string. But there's no need to stock the exploratorium with a hobby collection from each child. An even better bet is a selection from the home "junk box" or "junk drawer" into which even the youngest child tends to toss varied minor treasures. Suggest that the children bring these collections, intact, to class. The chance to pore over someone else's junk has some of the learning qualities of an archaeological dig.

• **Collective collections** require a theme set or a question posed by either the teacher or a children's committee. The chosen theme, approved by the class as a whole, could be as specific as "Vitamins" or "All About Mexico." Too narrow an idea, however, may mean a lost opportunity for kids to find their own ways of organizing a collecting experience.

Consider a theme such as "How We Observe Things." Students can provide a variety of lenses that are used to look at the world in different ways. Collection possibilities include eyeglasses, sunglasses, magnifying glasses, binoculars, stereopticons, telescopes, microscopes, kaleidoscopes, strips of colored plastic or cellophane, peepholes in cardboard, reflecting mirrors, and various kinds of bottles as viewers. Perhaps there's also room for things that *limit* seeing, such as blindfolds, sleep goggles, and blinders. (This can lead to a science-related lesson about observation and also can stimulate a writing lesson!) And think of the collecting and discovering possibilities opened up by questions such as "What makes noise?" or themes such as "Patterns," "Shadows," or "Lights and Colors." Collecting, after all, is a way to make perceptions possible, not a prescription for what to see and how to see it.

• **Rotating collections** are even more openended. The collection begins with one child's contribution. A second child contributes an item that seems related to the first in some way. A third student adds another related item and so on. (What might be added, for instance, if the first two items were a bubble-gum baseball card and a red-and-blue hair ribbon? a dog license and an income tax form? a soda-bottle cap and a padlock?) Classifying and sequencing skills are called into play here. Math teachers can formalize the teaching of these skills with attribute exercises in which kids see connections between such variables as color, shape, area, thickness, height, width, and so on. The rotating collection also allows children to practice and learn from rational thinking: Kids gain an awareness that things around them have many meanings, depending on the way they think about them.

The actual collecting should be easy for the kids to do. Kids should concentrate on collecting things they can accumulate in a short time, but they shouldn't inundate the classroom with stuff. One of the best ways to keep a collection manageable is to limit it to the confines of a shoe box, one per child. The box keeps both the size of items and the number of items in reasonable classroom scale. (The limit doesn't have to be too rigid; children who need a little more room can use a box that hiking boots come in.) For a class of 25, the shoe box collections stack neatly in just about 7 cubic feet of space.

Making sense of the collection

With their collections complete and their shoe boxes filled, the kids begin the next phase of

their work—making sense and excitement out of what they've collected. Unfortunately, children's chances to do basic sorting and organizing are often preempted in classroom activities. The child's lessons in classifying, for example, may involve pondering prescreened and very limited collections of things—words, colors, shapes, or whatever—and trying to arrive at the one predetermined "right" order.

Creating the exploratorium shouldn't become one more assigned task of moving from a fixed collection to fixed answers. The project can provide a kind of opportunity that kids may not have experienced before. Consider these two examples, set in the formal language of learning objectives:

1. Having made a collection of things, the child will demonstrate the ability to select, classify, and organize an element of the collection.

2. Given the ordinary classification for a collection of things, the student will supply at least one novel way to perceive the collection.

To meet such objectives—and progress toward the goal of making sense of the collections—students begin with some well-organized disorder. Define work areas as clearly as possible on desk or table tops or, better, on the classroom floor. This is especially important if individual collections are to be kept intact. Whole-class collections, however, can be freely dumped from the shoe boxes and thoroughly mixed before they are sorted out again. (Remember to have children label items they want returned.)

The classroom curators begin the defining-and-organizing phase of their work by exploring the many meanings and points of view inspired by a collection. For example, think about a shoe box full of matchbook covers collected by one child or by the class. How many matchbooks can be displayed, and how can they be arranged? Suggest a beginning list of variables, remembering again to let the children take over as quickly as possible. Such a list might include size, shape, color, strike-in-front, strike-in-back, geographical origin, advertising carried. Ask some questions; they might deal with the history of matchbooks, how they were first made and how they're made now, the dollar volume of business they represent, how they're bought and sold and given away, and the chances they'll be used in the future or be replaced by some other inflammatory device. From all such possibilities, what does the curator want to research and display?

Following the sorting and researching—after the kids have determined the kinds of information, insights, ideas, and experiences they wish to share—the curators must then decide how they'd like the exhibit to work.

How can they communicate their findings and open up opportunities for inquiry? Should the exhibit ask questions? Should it supply answers or just clues? (Perhaps the worst sort of exhibit is the kind that—like some textbooks—presents a closed circuit of questions and answers.) Must the exhibit be hands-off, or are there ways to make it hands-on?

Displaying collections

One of the simplest display ideas used by museums is the curator's selection of just one item from his collection as a focus of interest. In the classroom this single-item exhibit area could be as plain as a desk top, a space marked on the classroom floor with tape or chalk, or even one of the shoe boxes.

A single matchbook might be featured, accompanied by mysterious clues about its origin, condition, or history. A real attention-getter might be a lone "Whatsit" from a child's collection of junk. It might be a spare part of uncertain origin—the sort of puzzling bit that tends to hang around for years, unidentified, in most households. Or it might be a gadget whose function is likely to be unknown to the other children—an old-fashioned nonelectric toaster or one of those silly household tools that keep popping up in the markets and on television. What does a "Whatsit" do? The only labels needed for the exhibit may be a large cutout question mark and the familiar red arrow. This is the sort of exhibit that prompts questions without half trying.

Another simple medium for display is a corrugated paper carton with the top and front cut out. Carton displays can be labeled and draped as elaborately as the kids want, but plain boxes will do well enough. Exhibits such as the one that presents different means of seeing and observing, however, won't work if children can only look from a distance. If they're going to get the point, kids must try out the various materials. Order becomes a problem here, and the secret of achieving it is clear marking of the places from which items are taken and to which they must be returned. One pattern for this is a pegboard display that is marked with the outlines of various tools to show where each belongs.

Other kinds of exhibits suggest different inviting display media. Consider free-standing kiosks made from rolled corrugated paper or from paper drums sometimes available from companies in the community. Or hang exhibit items from strings attached to the classroom ceiling. Small things—such as coins, stamps, or matchbooks from a particular country—can fit into a "wallet museum" made from the folding plastic pockets commonly used to

One class' collection: From ideas to exhibits

Some Collection Ideas...
Buttons (size, color, shape, feeling, history, manufacturing, materials, substitutes)
Seashells
Political Buttons
Menus
Rocks
Pencils (biggest and smallest, softest and hardest, colors, advertising, uses)
Sounds
Bottle Caps
Autographs
Baggage Labels
Sugar Packets
Postcards
Textures
Fabric Swatches
Tree Leaves
Wildflowers
Corks
Nuts, Bolts, and Nails
A Time Capsule (to be opened at the end of the school year)
Knots (have plenty of rope for visitors to tie with)
Marbles

Color and Light
Buckles
Keys
Pets (ants, bugs, and caterpillars)
Maps (topographical, street, utility, transportation, aerial view, zoning, political district, boating chart)
Beads
Cash Register Slips

The Collection is Made By...
Individual Children
An Exploratorium Committee
All the Kids in the Class
Every Kid in Turn

And They Collect...
Any Musical Instrument That Fits Into a Shoe Box (harmonicas, toy pianos, tin flutes, whistles, music boxes, horns, clickers, bells)
Junk noisemakers (wooden blocks, tin cans, lengths of pipe or tubing, plastic or glass bottles, paper boxes, glass, seeds)

They Choose an Organizing Theme...
"Sounds: Sweet and Sour"
"Music for Everyone"
"Junk Music"
"Play a Tune"
"Hearing"

And Mount the Exhibit...
In Cardboard Carton Display Cases
On a Table Top
On Display Panels
In a Floor Area
On Strings Hanging from the Ceiling
In Take-Home Shoe Boxes

And Invite Visitors To...
Look and Read
Play the Instruments
Decide Which Sounds Best and Worst
Record Their Opinions About What Makes "Music" and What Makes "Noise."

display snapshots. Or how about a "walking museum"? Children like to wear patches, buttons, and sometimes autographs on their clothing. It's just one more step to wearing an exhibit, like those marvelous street vendors who carry their wares in multipocketed costumes. And don't forget the reliable shoe box. In addition to working well in the classroom, it travels well. Shoe box exhibits can be loaned to other classrooms, and they can also be carried home. Good ideas deserve to go places.

Far out and close up

Don't be timid about trying things that are somewhat "farther out," about moving students from familiar to foreign surroundings. Consider the novel walk-through environments featured in many museums today. Creating that kind of exhibit takes time but is not totally beyond the reach of classroom exploratorium curators with one ample corner available. What's it like to live in a tepee, a yurt, a cave, a space capsule, a bird's nest, or a chipmunk's hole? Ambitious kids can do some research and then build environments (not miniature models) that provide live-in experiences. Even better, perhaps, are reconstructions of almost inaccessible environments—the surface of Mars or the center of Earth—or totally imagined environments—a dragon's lair or a learning cubicle a hundred years from now.

Of course you need go no farther than the materials right in your classroom to find the most readily available and most involving collection of all: the personalities and experiences of the children themselves. Think of an exhibit about "Us: How We Are Alike and Different" as part of a social studies or human relations lesson. Each child can supply or draw collectibles such as these:

- Fingerprints (everyone's elbow prints, knee prints, and footprints are also unique)
- Handwriting samples (with each child writing the same passage)
- A strand of hair
- Tracing of a hand or foot
- Heroes (written about or drawn)
- Baby pictures
- Examples of favorite colors, flavors, possessions, and mementos of favorite places
- Wishes (written about or drawn)
- Comparisons ("I'm as tall as a parking meter, as wide as a wastebasket, and as heavy as 75 cans of Campbell's soup.")
- How would I look if...? ("...I had wheels?" or "...I had arms like the Incredible Hulk's?")

If student contributors are not identified, the collection has the element of a wonderful "Guess Who" exhibit. And there are many more exhibit possibilities, such as one dealing with body awareness. Mount a regular full-length mirror so that children can see themselves as they are. Then hang curved sheets of reflective Mylar so that they can see themselves in fantastic fun-house shapes.

Whether its exhibits run to the exotic or the familiar, whether its scale is giant or microscopic, the classroom exploratorium will serve a very special purpose: to provide a greater and more varied awareness of what the world is like. That kind of awareness doesn't often proceed from being told about it; it happens magically when children are encouraged to become actively involved.

Steven Caney, a designer and museum consultant, is the author of *Steven Caney's Playbook, Steven Caney's Toybook,* and *Steven Caney's Kids' America* (Workman).

MAINTAINING DISCIPLINE

6
MAINTAINING DISCIPLINE

Today's teachers commonly form strategies for controlling students' behavior in the classroom that encourage students' self-control. This usually implies that the teacher imposes the necessary ground rules but the students take responsibility for their own learning by governing their own classroom behavior. In this chapter, experienced teachers offer practical suggestions and share the methods that have helped them maintain discipline in their own classrooms.

Three-dimensional discipline: Rules by consensus

Few sane people would pick a fight if they were outnumbered 25 or 30 to 1; yet that's close to what most teachers do when they adopt a traditional plan of classroom discipline. The guiding "them against me" philosophy guarantees a no-win situation.

It doesn't have to be that way. Discipline can be a shared, even-handed responsibility developed and administered as part of a classroom social contract. Such a contract is produced through a process called Three-Dimensional Discipline, which is based on prevention, action, and resolution. The social contract consists of three kinds of rules and their consequences, all of which are generated, discussed, tested, and refined by members of the class:

1. The teacher develops rules for the students and proposes consequences—not "punishments"—appropriate for violations of the rules.

2. Students develop rules for the teacher and consequences for violations of those rules.

3. Students develop rules for themselves and consequences for violations of those rules.

The process is time-consuming and can at times be tedious. But the product—a statement that reflects the needs of all persons in the classroom—is well worth the effort. The contract saves time in the long run because it tends to be a guide to civil behavior—and a means of preventing bad behavior—rather than a mere schedule of violations and penalties.

The first rule: Make good rules

Make your rules as specific as possible. A detailed list of rules about things that really matter is more effective than one global rule whose vagueness masks many areas of doubt and confusion. Make your rules positive by stressing acceptable behavior. For example, "Settle disputes by talking rather than by fighting" is a better rule than "No fighting."

Also, by distinguishing between *punishments* and *consequences,* you ensure that students understand the relationship between a violation and what follows. Punishments are designed merely to "get even" or to hurt the offender; they have little to do with the behavior involved. For example, traditionally, if Johnny throws paper on the floor, he is punished with some form of silent detention. Experience indicates that such punishments do not produce long-term changes in behavior. Consequences, on the other hand, are designed to correct rule-breaking behavior quickly and directly. Consequences for throwing paper might be picking up the paper, apologizing to the teacher and the class for the specific misbehavior, and possibly—if the offense warrants—tidying up the classroom still further. It is particularly important for students to understand that consequences are not a matter of the teacher "getting even," but rather a group's way of "undoing" inappropriate behavior.

Teachers make rules for students

The teacher brainstorms a comprehensive list of rules as part of the raw material from which the social contract will be developed. These rules must, of course, fit under the umbrella of existing federal, state, local, and school regulations. Within those bounds, the teacher should try to draft rules about matters that are personally important, as well as rules to meet the needs of the class as a whole. Examples of such rules are "Homework must be turned in on the day it is due" and "Students will be on time for class." Achievement—how much and how fast students learn—is not a proper subject for general rule-making, but the teacher's rules should otherwise cover every aspect of classroom behavior and study habits. Bear in mind that these rules will be understandable and enforceable only if they are specific. If general rules leave room for doubt and interpretation, discipline is likely to collapse.

After establishing clear, specific rules, the teacher must develop consequences for violations of each rule. Students should know that there will be no allowance for mitigating circumstances (for example, the teacher will not overlook the violation even if Mary forgets her homework for the first time ever or when John acts up after coming back from three days sick in bed). Exceptions to the rules invite manipulative behavior, excuse thinking, and the whining "I didn't mean it" that teachers of young children have grown to dread.

The teacher, on the other hand, should not box herself in with a short list of unjustifiably harsh consequences. A range of alternatives, with at least one that falls in the warning or stop-and-think category, can help the teacher avoid this problem: Within a range of alternatives, any one consequence can be implemented at the teacher's discretion. Or a posted hierarchy of consequences can make clear what will happen each successive time a rule is violated; for example, for violating the rule, "Students will arrive for class on time," the consequences might be:

- The first infraction results in a teacher-student conference.
- The second infraction results in the student attending an afterschool class to make up the lost time.
- The third infraction results in a parent-student-teacher conference to find ways that the student can get to class on time.

Such a sequence offers the teacher less discretion, but the consequences are uniform, and everyone knows in advance exactly what will happen each time a rule is violated.

It may be helpful to have a system of positive consequences (free time, preferred activities, reduced homework, etc.) for students who consistently follow the rules. Some teachers, fearing that this practice creates an environment in which good behavior must be "bought," feel that it is wrong to reward expected behavior. Providing positive consequences, however, can prevent good students from developing the attitude that "the only way to get attention is to act out."

Students make rules for the teacher

Rule-making offers students a chance to express their feelings about the range and the limits of the teacher's behavior. It enables them to feel that they have at least some control over what happens in the classroom.

Student rule-making for the teacher will vary depending on the students' age, grade, and the kind of classroom—single subject or self-contained—in which they work. The teacher may choose to start the social contract process by reading a list of proposed rules and consequences for students, carefully explaining how each one helps maintain a supportive, productive classroom environment. The teacher might then present examples of two or three kinds of rules that students can make for the teacher before inviting students to compose a full complement of policies.

The teacher might also choose to reverse these steps, encouraging students to develop rules they think should be obeyed by a fair and supportive teacher before introducing the teacher-made rules.

In either case, students' proposals, like those of the teacher, must be consistent with existing federal, state, local, and school rules. This safeguards against the listing of such rules as "Students can smoke in class whenever they want" and other equally unrealistic measures. Students will accept this limit more easily if they understand that the teacher's rules follow the same guidelines.

Have students generate their rules by brainstorming. They should feel free to propose any rule that seems important and that does not violate existing laws and regulations. Help create an atmosphere in which everyone is comfortable making suggestions. Students should not fear that their ideas will seem silly or impractical to the teacher or to fellow students.

Students might make the rule, "The teacher must give all homework for the upcoming week on the Friday before so that students can plan their weekly work schedules." They would impose one of the following consequences, written specifically for this rule, if the teacher committed a violation:

HOW TO MAKE SURE YOU'RE HELPING YOUR STUDENTS

When implementing a classroom program based on reality therapy, ask yourself the following questions to make sure you're helping students.

1. Stay involved with students.
• Do I spend time having fun with students?
• Have I stopped threatening, using sarcasm, and other failure-breeding habits that break down relationships?
• Can I tell when a student is testing me to see if I'll give up or get angry?
• Do I try to work with students when they're upset? When I'm upset?
• Do I get involved with a child only when I'm upset with his behavior?

2. React only to current behavior.
• Do I avoid using past failures to "put down" a student?
• Am I careful to ask "What," not "Why"?

3. Get students to evaluate themselves.
• Am I guiding the student to evaluate his own behavior instead of just telling him the behavior is wrong and that he must change it?

4. Help students make plans to change behavior.
• Is the plan specific?
• Is it reasonable?
• Is it short?
• Does it help build feelings of confidence and self-worth?
• Does it avoid resentment?

5. Respond to student commitment.
• Do I check up on the student's commitment and give him a word or sign of encouragement?

• Do I respond regularly—not only when the child has failed?

6. Accept no excuses.
• Do I ask "What are you going to do now?" instead of "Why did (or didn't) you do that?"

7. Avoid punishments.
• Am I careful to ensure that plans focus on changing behavior and on improvement—not on retribution?
• When a student doesn't meet his plan, do I focus on "recycling" that plan into one that works, instead of abandoning it in exasperation?

8. Don't give up.
• Am I willing to go back to step one and start again, if a child isn't ready to make a plan to change?
• Am I willing to keep trying just a little longer than the child thinks I will?

- The teacher can give only four days of homework, none for the weekend.
- The teacher cannot give any homework that week.
- All homework is optional for extra credit.
- Students can choose their own homework assignments for the week.

Students make ✓ rules for themselves

The students, who by now should be well acquainted with the process, develop a list of rules and consequences that define acceptable and unacceptable behaviors for themselves.

For violating the rule, "Name calling, use of four-letter words, and use of put-downs are *not* allowed," possible consequences might be:

- The student must make a public apology.
- The student must write a letter of apology.

Violation of the rule, "Permission must be asked of others and granted by them before anyone can borrow items that belong to them," might result in one of the following consequences:

- The borrower must return the borrowed item.
- The borrower must loan the student something of the student's choice for one day.
- The borrower must pay rent, but no more than 25 cents a day.

Working for consensus

All efforts up to this point involve production of raw materials from which the social contract will be forged. The first step in evaluating these raw proposals is to make sure all students understand the implications of the rules and their consequences and how these implications might affect classroom life. Role-playing different rule-violation situations is a good way

to demonstrate the relationship of rules and consequences to an orderly, functioning classroom.

The social contract is made up of rules and consequences endorsed by either the whole class or a great majority of it. During the final negotiation of the social contract, the teacher may serve as "the authority" or as an equal group member. The role of group member—maintaining control only to see that the decision-making process works effectively—is obviously more attractive. The teacher, however, will ultimately have to live by the contract and be responsible for its implementation; so if there are rules and consequences that the teacher cannot accept and must veto, they should be dealt with at the outset of the class discussion. The fewer vetoes exercised the better, though, because mutual trust in the process is greatly influenced by the teacher's willingness to go along with the rules and consequences that are agreed to by the class. Announce that the contract will be "on trial" for a month or so and that modifications and changes can occur at the end of that time. Because an inappropriate rule or consequence can be eliminated on the basis of real data at that time, the teacher is able to avoid vetoing proposals that will clearly prove to be unworkable. Test as many rules and consequences as possible in the classroom.

Final agreement on the rules and consequences of the social contract is best reached in three stages:

1. Seek unanimous consent. Some rules and consequences will be readily accepted by the whole group the first time the class goes through the list.

2. For all remaining rules, try to obtain a consensus through debate and discussion. Many more rules and consequences will be

approved this way. A second opportunity for a consensus decision may be evident when discussion ebbs and differences appear minimal. The teacher may then say, "I can see that most of you want this rule, and I wonder if anybody who does not would really object to trying it for about a month to see what happens." If strong objections reappear, a consensus is not possible.

3. Vote to determine inclusion or exclusion of the remaining rules. The suggested models are the U.S. Senate treaty-ratification vote or the U.S. House of Representatives impeachment vote, either a two-thirds or three-fourths majority, to ensure that most students will abide by the rule or consequence.

Testing for commitment

Some of the prime reasons that students break rules are that they do not understand them, they do not know they exist, or they "play ignorant." Extensive discussions help ensure that each student understands all the rules and consequences proposed and makes intelligent, informed choices. One additional step can make certain that real or "play" ignorance is not a cause of discipline problems. A written test will measure whether or not students understand the social contract. Like any other test, it should match the age and abilities of students. Either a perfect or a near-perfect score is required for students to pass the test.

The final step in the social contract process is to design and display a poster or bulletin board that clearly states each rule and consequence—preferably signed by all students and the teacher.

Most teachers who have implemented social contracts report significant decreases in the amount of instructional time that they spend attending to discipline problems. Although the social contract process may be initially time-consuming and sometimes tedious, it is likely to be worth all the time and energy put into it. The social contract is a vehicle for making classroom rules explicit and for inviting students to become part of the process. The teacher, then, is not the only person in the classroom dealing with discipline problems; all discipline problems are shared by everyone in the class, and resolution occurs through participation. Such shared responsibility is a good way to tackle, and to subdue, the discipline problems in any classroom.

Richard Curwin, the chairperson of teacher improvement programs at the National Technical Institute for the Deaf in Rochester, N.Y., and **Allen Mendler,** a certified school psychologist in the Rush Henrietta New York School System, are the authors of *The Discipline Book: A Complete Guide to School and Classroom Management* (Reston Publishing Co., 1980). **Barry Culhane** is a professor of psychology at the National Technical Institute for the Deaf, Rochester Institute of Technology.

Encouraging responsibility

This discipline plan, based on William Glasser's reality therapy, helps students learn self-control and responsibility, decreases discipline referrals, and helps teachers' morale.

Here's a typical scene in an elementary school:

As the fifth grade finishes a writing assignment, Ms. Jackson notices a wad of paper flying through the air and eyes the person who threw it.

Ms. Jackson: "Leslie, please stop." Two minutes later, Leslie throws another wad of paper. Ms. Jackson approaches her desk to speak with her privately.

Ms. Jackson: "Leslie, what are you doing?"

Leslie: "Who, me?"

Ms. Jackson: "Yes. What are you doing?"

Leslie: "Nothing."

Ms. Jackson (calmly): "Please, Leslie, I just asked what you were doing."

Leslie: "I guess I threw something."

Ms. Jackson: "Is that helping you?"

Leslie: "Yes. I'm finished with my work, and I'm bored."

Ms. Jackson: "Is it helping the other people in the class?"

Leslie: "No, I guess not."

Ms. Jackson: "Is what you're doing against the rules?"

Leslie: "I only threw two. Harold threw one first."

Ms. Jackson: "Is what you did against one of the seven school rules posted on the wall?"

Leslie: "Yes, but I was bored."

Ms. Jackson: "I'd like you to sit in the time-out chair by the bookcase and think of a plan for solving this problem. When you have a plan, bring it to me so we can talk about it. Then you can rejoin the class."

Leslie did come up with a plan. She told Ms. Jackson, "From now on, I'll get a good book out of the library, so whenever I finish my work early I'll have something to do."

This scene is typical of what happens at the Lincoln School in Lincoln, Vt., an elementary school that has used the reality therapy discipline approach for the past 6 years. Although no discipline approach works for every child, the staff at Lincoln School is happy with this system, developed by psychiatrist William Glasser.

What makes it different?

Traditional discipline systems, which are based on threats and punishments, make *adults* responsible for kids' behavior. Reality therapy teaches children to be responsible for themselves and their own behavior. At its heart is the notion that children must learn to recognize behavior that hurts themselves or others, then make specific plans to solve their behavior problems.

Once a year, teachers attend an inservice workshop to review, evaluate, and refine the program. They discuss what has worked and what hasn't. They role-play actual situations and talk about how best to handle them.

Implementing reality therapy

Keith Hall, former superintendent of the district that includes Lincoln, credits reality therapy—and the staff's commitment to it—for turning the school around. "In the 5 years before we tried the Glasser approach," remembers Hall, "Lincoln was a school in trouble. Teachers came and went at an alarming rate. We had four different principals in 5 years. I don't think we had more discipline problems than any other school, but the atmosphere wasn't healthy. It wasn't positive."

When Phoebe Barash was hired in 1980 to be Lincoln's teaching principal, she'd had experience with reality therapy as a teacher in North Carolina. She proposed using the approach throughout Lincoln. Once the school board and the superintendent gave their nod, the staff of the school, guided by Barash, studied the Glasser approach and adapted it to Lincoln's needs.

They began with the premise that school should be a "good place" with reasonable rules—a place where students have a chance to be heard. So they first developed seven school rules, wrote them in a positive way (using "do's" instead of "don'ts"), and posted them throughout the school:

1. Keep hands, bodies, and objects to yourself.
2. Listen to the adult in charge.
3. Walk while inside the building.
4. Use acceptable language.
5. Use indoor voices.
6. Stay in your assigned area.
7. Leave gum and sharp objects at home.

The staff also adopted the practice, suggested by Glasser, of holding class meetings in each grade at least once a week—every day, if possible. "Class meetings are an essential part of reality therapy," says Barash. "Children frequently misbehave to get attention. They act up a lot less when they know that every day, in class meeting, they'll be able to talk and that the teacher and the rest of the class will listen."

Breaking a rule

When a student breaks a rule, his teacher asks the following series of questions, adapted from

Glasser's recommendations:

1. What are you doing?
2. Is it helping you?
3. Is it against the rules?
4. What will you do to change that?

Consistency is one of the keys to making reality therapy work, so the entire staff at Lincoln—including teachers, cooks, playground aides, and bus drivers—has learned to ask these questions when a child breaks a rule. The questions help the child judge his own behavior and devise a simple plan to change.

In class, if a student breaks his plan, the teacher accepts no excuses—these take away responsibility. Instead, she asks the questions again and tells the student to make a written plan.

Teachers encourage students to write plans themselves—to work on discovering their own ways to behave appropriately. Younger children, who are new both to writing and plan-making, may need guidance. But as children become more familiar with the approach, they get better at developing plans.

Each plan includes a check-back time, when the student and teacher meet again (usually 2 or 3 days later) to evaluate the plan and decide whether it's working. At that point, they may agree to renew the plan.

In Leslie's case, she and Ms. Jackson agreed at check-back time that the library book solution was working and that Leslie would continue to keep a good book at her desk. If the plan hadn't worked, Leslie and Ms. Jackson would have searched for a better one.

If a child breaks a written plan, he goes to the "planning room"—at Lincoln School, this is the principal's office. The principal asks the child to write a specific plan, including steps for following it and consequences for failing to meet it. For example, if a child has been fighting on the playground, the steps in his plan might include counting to 10 or speaking to the adult in charge whenever he gets so angry he wants to hit someone. The consequences of breaking the plan might be staying in from recess for a specified time.

Sometimes parents become involved when a student goes to the planning room. The principal calls them or asks the student to call or write a note to them, explaining what has happened and his plan to improve his behavior.

Types of class meetings

Class meetings are designed to foster communication and problem-solving skills. They're kept short for young students (10 to 30 minutes) but can be longer for older students (30 to 45 minutes). One type of class meeting focuses on class problems—including those caused by individual students. The teacher encourages students to discuss the problems openly and suggest solutions.

In another type of class meeting, the teacher selects a problem that's relevant to the students and asks open-ended questions. (Sometimes students suggest topics themselves.) These could include problems in the schoolyard, fairness in sports, friendship, democracy, and so on. If students suggest a trivial topic, the teacher can guide them toward applying it to more complex situations. The purpose is not to get kids to parrot "correct" answers but to help them develop thinking skills.

In a third type of meeting, the teacher uses a topic the students are studying as a springboard to discussion. For example, a factual question such as "What is the Constitution?" can introduce a meeting that explores what rights students have. Again, the purpose is to stimulate thinking and communication. Teachers in these meetings aren't just seeking the "right" answer but are accepting all opinions, because they indicate how well students understand the facts they've been studying.

Evaluating reality therapy

A survey of 22 elementary and junior-high schools from all areas of the country reported the following trends after using reality therapy:
• a 5 percent to 80 percent decrease in discipline referrals to the principal
• a 20 percent to 50 percent decrease in "second-time offenders" at the elementary level; a 5 percent to 72 percent decrease at the junior-high level
• a decrease in fighting—10 percent to 80 percent at the elementary level and 25 percent to 95 percent at the junior-high level
• an improvement in teacher morale.

What do teachers think?

The teachers at Lincoln School are enthusiastic about reality therapy, though they agree it's taken some getting used to. Teacher Marge Hill believes that the system has made children more responsible for themselves but says it takes a lot of time. "You frequently can't just handle a problem on the spot. You have to arrange a time to meet with the student to talk about the problem. Sometimes you can do that during class while the other children are working at their desks. Sometimes you can handle it in class meeting; sometimes you can't. It isn't always easy to find the time that this approach requires."

"The system doesn't fit some teachers' styles," says Vicki Greenhouse, who teaches second and third grades. "Some teachers feel it's a lot easier just to make a kid copy a page from the dictionary than to ask the questions and do all the talking and counseling that reality therapy requires. But it *does* make kids more aware of their own behavior and its consequences. Also, kids and their parents become involved in solving behavior problems. That's a big advantage."

Dexter Horton, who teaches grades five and six, emphasizes the importance of parental involvement in the plan-making system. "For a minor infraction in the classroom, the Glasser approach works well, handled by the student and teacher alone. But when the child goes to the planning room, the success of the system depends heavily on the parents' attitudes. If the parents support the plan, it works. If the parents don't care, the system breaks down and it's that much harder to produce an effective plan.

"The nature of the whole process often wins parents over, though. In any conference with a child, we first emphasize his strengths. When parents see that the teacher recognizes a child's good points, they often come to support a plan to help work on the child's weaknesses."

Many parents like the plan-making system because they believe it helps their children. "The system has given my son the opportunity to talk about what bothers him and, most important, makes him really look at what he does and how it affects other people," says one parent. A third-grader echoes that view: "I think it's good to make plans because when you sit down and have to answer all those questions about what you did and if it's helping you, it gets all your madness out."

Not everyone involved with the Lincoln School supports the plan-making system. As one school board member said, "Don't get me wrong—the system works. But I don't like it because I think it should be up to the teacher to discipline a kid."

One parent expresses her reservations about reality therapy this way: "I'm glad they're using the system at Lincoln. It suits them and has made huge improvements in the school. But I don't know if the system itself has done this. I think just about any discipline system can work if it's used with love and consistency, and any system will break down without those things."

Time well spent

Some might argue that reality therapy takes up too much valuable class time. Barash answers these critics this way: "Traditional discipline approaches take time too, especially because they often don't work and teachers have to keep repeating the same steps over and over again. They frustrate themselves and make students feel bad. Reality therapy *does* take time, but learning to behave appropriately is an integral part of a child's education. This approach puts learning self-control and responsibility at the hub of the school's curriculum, which is where we think it belongs."

Nancy Cornell, a former teacher, is now a free-lance writer.

Classroom rights and discipline

After studying and trying a multitude of disciplinary techniques, I've come to two conclusions:

1. If your gut reaction to a technique is negative, don't try it. You'll do yourself and the students more harm than good.

2. If you can't be consistent with one technique after 2 weeks of using it, then forget it. Being an effective classroom manager doesn't mean you have to grit your teeth and suffer.

Because I was either negative or inconsistent with every technique I tried, I finally developed my own. It involves four rules of order, plus the procedures to follow when these rules are broken. It's a simple system that starts with the teacher and extends to the students. Here's how my system works.

First, I list on the chalkboard the four rules, which I call "class rights." They are:

1. I will be listened to.
2. I will be respected.
3. I will be taken seriously.
4. I will be expected to take responsibility for my actions.

These rules don't emerge out of class discussion or consensus. They're *my* rules, and I present them as such. The kids don't seem to mind.

What the rules mean

Next, I explain the rules. I don't want to lose the group's cooperation here by being long-winded or overly descriptive, so I keep my explanation brief, firm, and objective:

• Rule 1 means that when one person's talking, the rest of us will listen.

• Rule 2 means we won't make fun of anyone.

• Rule 3 means anyone can ask any question without fear that it's "dumb" or that others will laugh.

• Rule 4 means every action has its consequence, and the consequence is related to the action.

I stress that the rules benefit everyone— students and teacher— because they ensure a classroom climate in which learning can take place.

After I've explained the rules—sometimes *while* I'm explaining the rules—I refer to them to correct any misbehavior or interruption. "Paul," I'll say, "read Rule 2 to yourself." I don't wait, stare, and make him wriggle on the hook; I just refer him to the rule. If he misbehaves again, I remind him: "Paul, read Rule 2 again and think about what it means." I'm careful not to lose my objectivity or to force Paul and me into a win-lose situation.

Next I explain that when students do something that compromises the rights of others, they must change their behavior. To make sure they understand this, I'll quietly ask the student after each reminder, "Do you know what you did and what not to do now, or would you like further clarification?" By doing that, I avoid confrontations and drawn-out discussions of the student's behavior. (After class, I note each misbehavior and reminder on an index card. This helps later if I need to involve parents in changing their child's behavior.)

"Three reminders, then..."

Finally, I tell the students they're allowed three reminders. Being reminded more than three times indicates a need for "after-school help." I don't explain what that means. Invariably, I'll have the first test case within 2 weeks.

I avoid labeling the after-school help a detention or punishment. When I notify the parents—usually the same day—that their child's staying for a conference, I simply say, "Mrs. Jones, Paul will be 30 minutes late coming home today. He and I need to discuss different ways of handling situations." At the conference, I maintain a calm tone, reminding myself that Paul has misbehaved, not committed a crime.

Paul appears indifferent—other students may appear defiant or (if they're in a hurry to get out) overly compliant. I don't acknowledge these attitudes. My purpose is to get the student to objectively describe five things:

- his misbehavior
- the effect on others when he acts that way
- the consequences to himself if he continues his misbehavior
- the effect his misbehavior has on me and my behavior
- alternative behaviors that would have more acceptable consequences for him.

I steer the conversation away from blaming others or dissecting the situation in which the student misbehaved. That way, he must take responsibility for his own actions. I resist the urge to tell him what his faults are, to wiggle my finger at him, and to send him off with a good talking-to. That way, he must do the work of changing his behavior. By taking responsibility for his own actions, he assumes more control over his own life; by doing the work of changing his behavior, he becomes more inner-directed.

Be realistic about change

After we've discussed alternative behaviors and their consequences, I let Paul choose which behaviors he'll try—but with one proviso. "They must be realistic," I tell him. "Better to succeed with small steps than to fail with large ones. I don't want you to get discouraged." I also emphasize realism in the consequences of his new behavior. He shouldn't expect that he'll become my prize pupil if he stops cutting up; nor can I expect that someone who's the class clown will suddenly become totally serious.

Part of the plan is that I will help with his new behavior, though I decide what I'm willing to do. I might offer him options for when he tries out his new behavior: I'd be willing to smile, wink, send home a "happy note," or let him accumulate points toward a reward—perhaps an assignment he wants to undertake. When he falls back into his old misbehavior, I'd be willing to call his name, rap on the desk, or hold up one finger. Even if he suggests it, I won't do anything that's inconsistent with my usual behavior (for example, singling him out for praise when he behaves well, or hitting him with a ruler when he misbehaves).

Once we agree on what he and I will do, we put this in writing and both of us sign the agreement. At this point, neither of us can renege. Paul must now take a copy of the plan home, discuss it with his parents, and return it to me with their signatures.

Enforcement is crucial, and I'm the one who must carry it out. If Paul or I find that the arrangement isn't working, either of us can call for a change. But until that happens, we must stick to what we agreed on, no matter what.

What about backsliding?

If Paul decides to return to his old misbehavior, we repeat the process: three reminders, and it's time for a conference. At the second conference, though, I'll have more to say. I'll describe my feelings, my options, my goals, and the resulting consequences.

My feelings might be that I'm dismayed because he frustrates my efforts to teach and the other students' efforts to learn. I make clear, though, that he's not responsible for my feelings—I don't want him changing his behavior just to soothe *me*. Rather, he's responsible just for his own actions, and for changing those actions for *his* own benefit.

My options might include punitive detention, parent conferences, a change of seats, or removal of class privileges.

My goals will be minimal changes in his behavior. These could mean that he will sit quietly while I'm giving instructions. Or that he will pass items by hand, not throw them.

My description of the consequences will be reasonable. If he changes his behavior, I'll have time to help him individually, or I'll allow him to talk under specific circumstances.

At this point, Paul and I draw up a new agreement and sign it. This time, the agreement includes the reasons why the first one failed. Like the first one, it needs his parents' signatures.

Create a positive climate

I've used this approach to discipline in traditional and open classrooms. I've found that not only does it work, it also creates a climate for positive group pressure; students feel more united when they're maintaining their own rights.

In fact, students eventually take over enforcing the rules—which is fine, because I can't guard everyone's rights. All they need to say is, "Nancy, Rule 1." in a calm, objective way. The statement isn't accusatory, just an observation. And it doesn't get the two students involved in arguing over particulars.

Perhaps the most satisfying aspect of this discipline system is that it benefits everyone, so everyone supports it. Even the shiest and most insecure student can point out an infraction and know that the others will back him up.

That's my system of discipline. If your gut reaction is positive, and you feel you can remain consistent, I think you'll find it creates a favorable classroom climate, one that you and your students will appreciate.

Katy Ridgley, formerly a junior-high teacher, is now a counselor at Townsend Middle School, Tucson, Ariz.

10 steps for controlling the disruptive student

Tommy is your discipline problem. It's now December, and despite frequent conferences with the principal, the school psychologist, and Tommy's parents, nothing seems to work.

Perhaps Tommy comes from a broken home or has a physical handicap; perhaps he is an only child or the last of a large family. It's likely that he has barely learned to read. He may never have had a consistently good school experience. But whatever his problems, you have him in your class for a school year, and if you can't get him to cooperate, he will suffer and your life will be miserable.

Here are 10 steps to follow in dealing with your behind-in-his-work, disruptive, doesn't-listen, never-on-time, always-picking-fights Tommy (or Susan). I believe if you doggedly follow them, you may help him change into someone who, though far from perfect, is enough improved to reward your efforts. No miracles will occur; this is hard, slow work. A month is probably your minimum time commitment; certainly you're not likely to see progress before that. But if the slow progress tempts you to give up, consider this question: What do you have that's any better?

1
List your no-nos

What you are doing with him now isn't working. This isn't criticism; your techniques may have worked with others. But if they haven't worked with Tommy by now, they probably aren't going to, so it seems only logical to change your approach. To start, sit down tonight in a quiet place and jot down the essence of what you do when Tommy upsets you. Forget the things you might have done or wanted to do. Do you talk to him? Yell at him? Threaten him? Ignore him? Have you asked him what's bothering him or how he feels? Be honest and list the pattern of the efforts you are making to help him right now.

For the next 4 weeks, try to refrain from doing anything you have put on tonight's list—unless it coincides with one or more of these 10 steps. When you are tempted (and you will be) to return to old patterns, pull out the no-no list and ask yourself: "If they didn't work in the past, what chance do they have now?"

2
Start fresh

Now promise yourself that tomorrow, no matter how disruptive Tommy is, you will try to act as if this is the first time he has behaved badly. Don't say, "OK, you're doing it again" or "I have had enough of that." Don't do anything that reminds him that this is repetitive behavior. On the other hand, if he does do something good, whether he's done it before or not, reinforce him: "Tommy, it's great when you sit still" or "I appreciate that." Tell him he was good, pat him on the head, give him some verbal and even physical recognition for good behavior. If you'll start fresh with him tomorrow and each day for the next month, you may be pleasantly surprised.

3
A better day tomorrow

This gets harder. I want you to figure out at least one thing you can do for Tommy, to Tommy, about Tommy that can help him have a better day tomorrow. It doesn't have to be much; a little goes a long way. One thing I have seen and done that fills the prescription is to pat him on the back as soon as he comes in and say, "Good to see you, Tommy." This brief greeting can be amazingly effective. Twenty seconds of unexpected recognition can mean a lot to him. Yes, he may wonder if you've suddenly gone crazy, but he'll still appreciate the simple, warm gesture. (And it will probably make you feel better, too.)

Or maybe a note has to be run to the office. Though you never in a million years would have asked Tommy, how about trying it tomorrow? "Hey, Tommy, would you do me a favor and take this down to the office and then come right back?" Say it calmly and matter-of-factly as if he has done it many times before. He may astonish you.

Commit yourself to doing this or something like it each day for the next 4 weeks. You are trying to give Tommy a new idea: that he has some value in your class. His only recourse for recognition for far too long has been to disrupt. You are trying to break that cycle, and these first three steps are the way to start. Continue to implement them as often as possible in the next month; they are prerequisites for the steps that follow.

The first three steps suggested changing your attitude and resolving to start fresh. The next set of steps suggests nonpunitive responses to Tommy when he breaks the rules—at least nonpunitive in the sense that they eliminate emotion-laden blaming and threatening. Keep the tone cool and crisp until Tommy gives some recognition of the rules and makes some effort to comply; at the same time, continue the effort of the earlier steps to inject some warmth and recognition into his day.

4
Quiet correction

All too soon, you are almost certain to have a disruption. Despite some success with the first three steps, at some point, Tommy's going to mess up. I am sure that just mentioning this has you apprehensively nodding your head. Perhaps when you ask the class to line up he continues sitting at his desk, or for the hundredth time he messes with the paints and spills some on the floor. Let's say this time he busts the line to find the place he wants and starts a fight in the process. Try to act as if it is the first time he has ever done this (step two) and ask him to stop fighting and go to his place in line. If this doesn't work, then try the scenario that follows, no matter what he replies or doesn't reply.

You: What did you do, Tom?

Tom: What?

You: What did you do, Tom?

Tom: Nothing.

You: Please Tom, I just asked you what you did. Tell me.

Tom: Well, this is my place in line and they won't let me in.

You: What did *you* do, Tom?

Tom: It's my place so I pushed my way in.

Then, with no further discussion, you take him by the hand and walk him to his correct place, and stay with him, maybe still holding his hand.

You: Can you walk quietly now?

Tom: What are you going to do?

You: I just asked if you can walk quietly now; we'd all like lunch.

Tom: OK, I'll try.

If he doesn't agree to try, don't give up; you still have six more steps.

You are .trying to establish that, while he must take responsibility for doing something wrong, you are willing to correct him and that, if he accepts the correction, that ends it. Also, your calm demeanor suggests confidence in him. You are not blaming, not threatening or yelling, not doing any of the things you used to do. If step four works and he goes quietly, say nothing more about the incident except to give him a little reinforcement like a pat or "I was sure you could do it."

5
Make a plan

Unfortunately, we must anticipate that before long there may be a situation for which step four won't work. Try it first, but if it doesn't, here is the scenario for step five. Let's continue with the scuffle in line, but as you walk toward him, Tommy dashes to the playground. He was supposed to go with the class to the cafeteria and he knows he's breaking the rules. But his need for attention is so great that he cares nothing about the rules. Your job is to get him to care, so get someone to take your class—perhaps appoint a monitor—and follow him, saying quietly, "Come here, Tommy, I want to talk with you." Don't chase, just walk quietly after him. When eventually you get to him:

You: Tom, what did you do?

Tom: I'm just swinging; I'm not hurting anybody.

You: Tom, where are you supposed to be?

Tom: Here; I'm not hungry anyway.

You: What's the rule?

Tom: I don't like that rule. Why should you have to eat if you're not hungry? Why can't I swing? There's no one here. Who'm I hurting?

You: Tom, was it against the rules? (Keep plugging away.)

You have to be very insistent. You are telling Tommy he broke the rules, and he is evading this issue in every possible way. Through all his evasions, you have to stick to a focus on rules. Ultimately, he will say, "Well, so what?" or he'll say nothing, which is a tacit admission that he is beginning to face the issue. Continue then:

You: Well, Tom, can you make a plan to follow the rules?

Tom: What do you mean? You mean go to lunch? Jeez, look how long the line is.

You: Are you willing to go to lunch? (Doggedly.)

Tom: What happens if I won't?

You: You'll have to leave the swings and take a rest. (To be explained.)

Tom: Do I have to go to the end of the whole line?

You: Not the whole line, just at the end of our class. After lunch, you can swing all you want.

I'm afraid I'll lose some of you here, because this takes time and, of course, it may not work. Or you'll worry that Tommy may think it's weak and silly. This early in the game, you may be right. But remember, you've admitted that what you usually do doesn't work. Besides, you're only at step five. It may work, and anytime something works, Tommy has had a success—and so have you. This is how he, how everyone, learns discipline.

6

Conference time

In steps four and five you were warm and supportive but did not talk much. Here, you bring Tommy to the point of a conference. Suppose you have trouble on the swings again: he won't take turns and kicks others away.

You: You want to use the swings, but we have rules. Can you make a plan with me so that you can get a fair turn on the swings and still give others their chance? You can't kick the others away.

Tom: Well, none of them like me; they never give me a turn. If I don't push, I never get a chance. You going to send me to the office?

You: No, Tom, I just want to make a plan with you. Let's try to work it out.

Tom: Heck, I don't like the swings much anyway. I like kickball but those rats never let me play.

You: That's funny; you used to play.

Tom: Yeah, but now they won't let me. They don't like me.

You: When you used to play, I heard them yell at you to follow the rules.

Tom: Big deal. I got mad once, and now they won't let me play.

You: I tell you what, Tom; why don't we take some time and maybe talk this all over. You're not having too much fun and I think I can help.

Tommy may be leery at first, believing that a conference just delays his ultimate punishment. All you can do is tell him he won't be punished and that you'd like to help him work it out. You listen to his complaints, talk, joke a little, get to know him better, and then try to work out a plan for him to follow the rules. Don't rehash old faults, but stress that rules are important and that

you have faith he can follow them. Finally you'll work out a plan either for the swings or to get him back at kickball. You may want to put it in writing; sometimes a contract helps the commitment. You're telling Tom that *he has the power to make a good plan.* It takes time, sure, but it takes a lot out of you to yell and get excited, too.

The last four steps are a graduated series of "benching" techniques. In effect, Tommy is interfering so seriously that he has to be taken out of the game to cool off. Once again, these steps come into play only if the earlier ones have failed; rather than acting out of instinct, you by now should have a rather clear idea that it's time to move to the next level of response.

7

Off to the castle

Now you need to create a place in your room where you can separate Tommy from the class. Not a dunce's seat or a punishment corner, this is an enrichment spot whose occupants can sit comfortably but separately from the class. Get together some books, coloring materials, puzzles, and quiet games, so that a child normally wouldn't mind being here for a while. Maybe you could discuss the idea in a class meeting and make a project out of it. This retreat is not only for disruptive children but also for others who need a quiet, separate place. However, the disrupters have priority in the "Castle" or whatever you decide to call it.

If Tommy disrupts, and you are by now sure none of the earlier steps are going to work, then say, "Look, Tom, go sit in the Castle." Don't do or say anything else. Take only a moment and send him firmly there, with no discussion. In the Castle, he can see and hear what's going on, but he is separated. Casually observe him, but pay no obvious attention to him. Don't worry if he spends several hours or most of the day there. The isolation has a way of making the normal class routines look more attractive. More important, *he has to learn that he can be nondisruptive,* and the way to learn is through experience.

Eventually, as nice as the Castle is, he'll want to rejoin the class. He may indicate his readiness by being a little restless. Don't take this necessarily as more disruption. Be ready to work out a plan. When you believe he has settled down, ask him if he is ready to return to his regular seat and take part. If he answers yes, then in your next break go over the class rules briefly and ask him to make a plan to follow them. The plan may be as simple as "OK, I'll try" or "If you seat me over there away from Johnny, we won't hassle so much." But he has to have some sort of plan.

Try to keep these mini-confrontations as light as possible. Laughter is a magic aid to this whole procedure. If you can keep your sense of humor, he'll have much less tendency to resist. When trouble arises, try to start with a step that will work at that time, but don't be too concerned at this stage if you think it right to start with the Castle. Don't be anxious to get him back to class. Count on the fact that he probably knows best what he can and can't handle. Again, be patient. You're trying to teach him something in a month that he hasn't yet learned in 5 years.

8
Off to the office

If Tommy still disrupts, despite steps one through seven, then he must be removed from class. You've put up with a lot, you've bent over backwards, but now you have had it. You can't continue to teach with a constantly disruptive child;

it's not fair to you or to the other children. When that point is reached, say, "Tom, go down to the office and take a rest." You take a rest, too. You've earned it.

Your principal must help you now in setting up the office rest place. Here again, it's a comfortable spot: perhaps an old donated couch the kids can scrunch down into. Have some books around, comic magazines, perhaps some peanuts or raisins for Tom and his confreres to munch on. In short, make him comfortable in an atmosphere that shows you care and that you don't want to hurt him.

This nonpunitive atmosphere may be hard for you and your principal to accept, but look again at that list from step one; you can see he's been in the "old" office plenty, with no results. Our task is to get him to change, and new surroundings as well as new methods are necessary. So get together with your principal and perhaps the rest of the faculty to establish this new office rest place. As with the Castle, it should be open to nondisruptive children as well, though Tommy has priority.

Here is sample dialogue from the office (almost repeating step seven):

Principal: What did you do, Tom?

Tom: Well, Miss Green kicked me out of the room. She's mean! I wasn't doin' nothing.

Principal: Well, this is what she said you did, here on this note.

Tom: Then what did you ask me for!

Principal: Because what you say is important. Look, let's work out a plan.

Tom: Oh, God, a plan. Is that all you do around here?

Principal: We always do it when you're here in the office.

Again, don't be punitive in act or demeanor. You, as principal, let him sit there comfortably while you get the facts. When he sees you're not about to paddle him or call his mother, he'll settle down. Once you have his story, move into the make-a-plan phase to get him back to class. If he complains about Miss Green and won't make a plan, tell him that it's his class and that, while you'll help him get along there, that's where he has to go. Let him sit there comfortably until he's ready to make a plan. Don't be concerned if he sits there a while. This whole scheme is aimed at reducing the alternatives, at getting him to realize that he really only has two choices: to be in class and behave, or to be outside and sit. Pretty soon, class will begin to look better, but he'll need some help with the plan. Help him. You're trying to convey to him that he has to follow reasonable rules, or he's out. But while he's out, you're not going to hurt him or reject him, which would let him rationalize his misconduct on the basis of his dislike for you.

9
A tolerance day

If he is totally out of control and can't be contained in the office rest spot, then a parent will have to be called in to take him home. This is the first time in this trial month you've contacted his parents (and if you follow steps one through eight, it shouldn't happen too often). Now is the time to put him on a "tolerance day," if possible. This means that he comes to school in the morning and stays until you've reached step nine. You don't have to start at one, but start as far back as you can. If he's quiet in the office, hold at step eight. Perhaps you or the principal could make a graph to show him his daily progress in tolerating more of school. But if he can't be helped in school at all, then he'll have to stay home, which means either a home tutor or, if no parents are at home, going on to step ten.

10
Where there's life there's hope

If school can't contain him, either he stays home or some other agency in the community will have to take him. Even juvenile hall is a possibility as a last resort. Though it sounds harsh, you must remember that sometimes this will finally jolt him awake, and he'll then be ready to plan. If he is in the hall, perhaps the judge can be persuaded to try letting him come back to school on a tolerance day from there. He can return from home, hall, or from any other agency if he seems ready, reentering at the lowest step possible depending on his behavior. Remember that step ten is for a very rare child, but when a child can no longer make it in school, this step must be used.

We all agree that discipline must be learned. I believe these steps outline an effective way to teach it early. The child who learns it very likely learns it for the rest of his life. As far as I'm concerned, there is no learning more valuable; steps like these should be built into the curriculum.

William Glasser, MD, is a psychiatrist and the author of several books on educational theory. He is the author of *Reality Therapy, Schools Without Failure,* and his most recent work, *Control Theory in the Classroom* (Harper & Row, 1986).

Reward direction, not perfection

Joe is the school bully. Although he is only in the fourth grade, he is big for his age. He picks several fights a day. His attacks are both physical and verbal, but his victims are always smaller and weaker than he is. He can skillfully trip a running classmate or "accidentally" push another child's face into the drinking fountain. He can spot another child's insecurity and tease cruelly ("Rachel's father ran away; Rachel's father wants to play").

When he was in the primary grades, his behavior was disturbing but didn't cause a school-wide commotion. Now it is one of the most frequent topics of conversation in the teachers' lounge. Of greatest concern to the staff is the fact that Joe's pugnaciousness does not seem to have been affected over the years by any method of punishment. Various teachers tried detention, suspension, disciplinary talks by the school principal, and exclusion from recess and lunch breaks. Nothing curbed his aggressiveness. Sensing the desperation of his fellow teachers, Mr. Firstyear agreed to try some of his newly learned behavior modification techniques with Joe. The rest of the staff applauded his willingness to tackle the problem but feared that his innovative strategies would be as abortive as their previous attempts. Many of them shared a deep-seated belief that Joe was a born troublemaker who was bound to end up in juvenile hall.

Spurred on by the challenge of the situation, Mr. Firstyear developed a plan to change Joe's highly undesirable behavior. He met with Joe, and they agreed on the following contingency contract: if Joe succeeded in not fighting during one week, on Friday he would earn a lunch-hour trip to the local hamburger restaurant accompanied by Mr. Firstyear. Both parties in the contract were satisfied with its conditions. Coming from a low-income family, Joe's excursions to restaurants had been highly infrequent. The prospect of leaving school to eat a hamburger with a teacher was especially motivating. Mr. Firstyear felt that a week without Joe's fighting would definitely be worth giving up his lunch hour on Friday. They agreed to put the contract into effect the next Monday.

The next week proved to be a disaster. Joe broke his contract the first day when he became upset in an afternoon ball game and pushed another boy down. The rest of the week got progressively worse. Realizing that he had lost his chance to go to lunch with Mr. Firstyear, Joe became more aggressive than ever before. What had gone wrong? Both Joe and the teacher had been so optimistic about the contract before the week began. Now Joe was frustrated and angry, and Mr. Firstyear felt he had failed hopelessly.

Mr. Firstyear deserves praise for his attempt at behavioral contracting. Despite the seeming fruitlessness of his effort, he did formulate an observable goal, include Joe in negotiating the contract, and select a highly appropriate reinforcer for the child. He made just two major errors: he tried to go too far too fast; and he did not help Joe structure an alternative activity to win recognition from his peers.

The goal was too difficult to attain in just one step. Consider the number of years Joe had spent building up his repertoire of aggressive acts. Consider the attention he had been given for his role as school bully. Hoping to reverse such a firmly entrenched behavior pattern with one no-fighting contract was an unreasonable expectation. A more successful strategy might have been to adopt a more gradual notion of goal attainment. A single 15-

minute recess without fighing might have constituted a more attainable goal than a one-week contract. Then gradually, if Joe were successful, the length of no-fighting time could be extended to one week.

The goal should include some positive acts for Joe to accomplish, not merely the absence of fighting. Mr. Firstyear could have helped Joe specify some alternative actions that would be incompatible with bullying. For example, Joe could have been assigned to protect a younger child; he could be rewarded for complimenting classmates for successes; and the time he spent in cooperative play or work activities could have been tallied and recognized. An instance of any one of these more constructive behaviors would be a sign of progress worthy of recognition.

Novice teachers hold no monopoly on perfectionist, all-or-none standards for behavior change. Mr. Firstyear is certainly not alone in his failure to set constructive step-by-step expectations for his pupil. If you're having trouble improving the behavior of your classroom troublemaker, maybe it's because you have unrealistic, all-or-none standards for behavioral change. Whether you're a novice or veteran teacher, you may be defeating your efforts with this perfectionist attitude.

The problem is a common one. Teachers strive to make progress with their students, to teach them all they can in the short time students are in class. Sometimes in their zeal teachers forget that success does not always come rapidly or all at once. The old Chinese proverb is pertinent: "A journey of a thousand miles begins with but a single step."

Instead of setting themselves and their pupils up for failure by expecting rapid improvements in behavior, teachers may need to begin looking for satisfaction from a series of slow but steady successes. Wouldn't it be preferable to set mini-goals that students have a high probability of attaining? Students might better reach their end goals and would enjoy success in school in the process.

The principle of successive approximations

The principle that summarizes learning as a series of small steps is called the principle of successive approximations.

Consider the way a new mother and father teach their baby to speak. They don't wait for the child to recite the Gettysburg Address before expressing pleasure at the child's accomplishment. Instead, they express genuine delight and give the child attention and positive reinforcement for an utterance as simple as "Da." As the child's vocabulary increases, their reinforcement, attention, and responsiveness are contingent upon the child's uttering increasingly complex ideas. No longer do they give any positive reinforcement for "Da."

This behavior is an excellent example of the principle of successive approximations. The child is allowed or induced to try the desired behavior and is progressively reinforced for attempts that come closer and closer to that behavior. Less desirable responses are simply ignored and tend to drop out.

Teaching a child to speak is relatively simple, because parents have mastered their own language sufficiently to measure their child's progress. The approximations to correct speech can be fairly easily identified. However, many educational goals are stated in ways that are difficult to break down into step-by-step sequences that can be successively reinforced. To make the principle of successive approximations work, the end goal needs to be broken into a series of prerequisite skills or component tasks. Let's look at some common behavior problems faced by teachers and see how the principle of successive approximations applies to them.

Application of the principle

A common example of a behavior to which the principle of successive approximations can be applied is the age-old problem of the student who calls out in class without raising his hand. In this case, the teacher's end goal is for the pupil to raise his hand quietly when he wants to talk and to wait to be recognized by name before he speaks out. Simple as this goal may sound, it too can be broken down into several steps. The child who has difficulty remembering to raise his hand in class might progress through a hierarchy of approximations similar to these before reaching the goal:

1. Calls out in class without raising his hand.

2. Calls out in class but raises his hand afterward.

3. Calls out in class while simultaneously raising his hand.

4. Raises hand, waits for 5 seconds, then speaks before being recognized.

5. Raises hand, waits for 30 seconds, then speaks before being recognized.

6. Raises hand, waits to speak until recognized by teacher.

If a child is at the first level on this hierarchy, it's progress if he moves to the second level. That is, if he never raises his hand, it's a step in the right direction for him to raise his hand at all, even if he does so after he has called out. The tendency toward improvement, no matter how slight, can be rewarded to promote further progress. It's difficult for some teachers to reward behaviors other than the one at the highest level since it means giving reinforcement for an improved behavior that is still *wrong*. As contrary as it may seem, we often achieve correct behavior by performing gradually less and less *incorrect* behavior. These approximations to the goal must be recognized so that the student learns he is making progress. The title of this article might make a useful slogan to remember: reward direction, not perfection.

The principle of successive approximations can be usefully applied to teach hundreds of behavioral skills. The above examples serve as just a starting point. The principle can be incorporated into all curriculum areas, academic as well as behavioral. For example, many teachers have received absolutely atrocious student papers on which they have hastily scrawled in big, bold letters, "Sloppy handwriting, do over neatly!" The student may be functioning at the lowest levels on the handwriting skills hierarchy, but with a response like that, the teacher gives him no hope of success in reaching higher levels. Perhaps a more appropriate way of evaluating his writing would be to circle the most clearly written word on the page and to indicate next to it: "This word is written neatly. It's easy to read. See if on the next paper you can make lots of words look as evenly spaced and on the line as this one." Then the next paper may contain several such clear words to circle. The strategy for each successive paper would be to praise handwriting examples that get progressively closer to the ideal.

Effects on teacher skills

The person who attempts to teach according to the principle of successive approximations learns to become a keen observer of student behavior. Observational skills are necessary because it is difficult to assess improvement if the student's present level of functioning is not known. Teachers who want to reinforce at the first sign of progress must know their students well. They learn to recognize growth quickly and offer support for it. They are constantly on the lookout for increasingly cooperative behavior from the aggressive student, initial social interactions from the withdrawn student, more polite language from the profane student, prolonged attention from the distractable student, and a more skillful move from the uncoordinated student.

In addition to becoming keen observers, teachers learn to be good task analyzers. Teachers who practice applying the principle of successive approximations are able to break a long-term goal into its component short-term parts. They can then reinforce these parts, treating them as mini-goals in themselves.

Criticisms of the approach

The principle of successive approximations is simple to talk about, but its application is anything but simple. Some teachers are wary of incorporating the successive approximations principle into daily practice. They cite several highly relevant criticisms that merit thoughtful consideration.

More work?

One criticism is often phrased in this way: "Observing where all my students are functioning and analyzing how to help them progress step by step to their goal sounds like a lot of extra work to me. How can a teacher with 30-plus students realistically do this?"

The number of hours devoted to professional work need not be any greater than before, but the way in which you spend those hours might be quite different. The problem is analogous to the Iowa farmer who complained, "I'm so busy chasing pigs that I don't have time to build a fence." Sometimes you become so accustomed to performing laborious but inefficient chores that you don't have time to structure a more effective learning environment.

Certainly it takes a great deal of time to prepare a lesson plan that is suitable even for the middle 50 percent of the students in a class. But one fourth of the students will find that material too difficult, and the other one fourth will find it too easy. The students for whom the material is not best may tend to become discipline problems or develop poor work habits and require further hours of teacher time and emotional energy.

All the work of individualizing instruction does not have to be performed by the teacher alone. It is possible to organize the classroom so that pupils who have already mastered a particular skill or concept can be assigned as assistant teachers to help pupils who are still learning. Such an arrangement produces educational benefits for the assistant teachers as well as for their students. Some schools organize parents as volunteer teachers' aides. These parents can be assigned to duties requiring individualized attention. Certain routine classroom chores can be delegated to students, thus lightening the teacher's load, teaching students a sense of responsibility, and contributing to others' welfare.

Too much at once?

The critic might well say: "You're setting an unreasonable goal if you expect me suddenly to change my way of doing things and to start preparing individual lesson plans for every single pupil. That's just too much. Who's guilty of advocating perfectionist standards now?"

No teacher is expected to individualize educational programs for each student overnight.

Such an expectation would be unrealistic, would set you up for failure, and would fail to incorporate the principle of successive approximations. Instead, you might set mini-goals for yourself. Your long-term target is to individualize educational experiences for all students. A first step in that direction is to individualize the education of one especially difficult-to-teach child. Or you might choose to try successive approximations with a small group of pupils in just one curriculum area. As you become more adept at observing student behavior and at analyzing component tasks, you can begin adding more students and/or curricula to individualizing efforts. Through this gradual approach you can eventually approach the mark: providing individually relevant education to all your students.

Lowers our standards?

A third common criticism of the proposed teaching strategy usually is presented like this: "It sounds to me as if teaching according to the principle of successive approximations means accepting mediocrity from my pupils. I expect written papers in which *all* words are neat, not just a few. I can't buy this approach if it means I have to lower my standards."

Apologies are in order if we have given the impression that you'll have to lower your end goals for your students in order to individualize their education. Your goals can and should remain high. To lose sight of your ideal destination would be a disaster. Conversely, to expect to reach any destination without traversing many intermediate points would also be a mistake. What must be changed, then, is not the end of the journey, but the starting point. And the starting point for any journey is your present location, not where you would like to be. The starting point for each student's

learning is what he can do now, not what he is "supposed" to be able to do.

Unequal treatment?

A fourth major concern that comes up frequently is the inequality teachers perceive to be implied in the successive approximations approach. As they express it: "But if one student gets the same reward for a top quality performance that another student gets for a poor quality performance, injustice is the result."

Be careful now about the term *justice*. Remember that the purpose of education is to help each pupil learn to the best of his ability. The most fair treatment then would be to arrange the educational environment so that every pupil is learning as fast as possible and feeling equally good about his progress. Nothing in this concept of equal education requires that every pupil study the same work at the same time. In fact, requiring identical performances for identical rewards is distinctly unfair.

What if health needs were met in this way? Suppose some bureaucrat figured that since the average American spends 4 days in the hospital each year, it should be required in the interests of equality that every American must spend 4 days in the hospital each year. Ridiculous, of course. But no more ridiculous than requiring every schoolchild to undergo the same educational treatment regardless of need. Just as individual treatment marks our approach to medical needs, so it should mark our approach to educational needs.

What about grading?

The question goes something like this: "In my school, I am obliged to fill out report cards with letter grades that are sent home to all the parents. How can I possibly give meaningful grades if my students are all working at different levels?"

If you're thinking in terms of traditional grading systems, you'll have problems because traditional grading systems are set up on a norm-referenced basis. That is, each student's performance in class is compared to every other student's performance. The norm-referenced system presupposes that all pupils in a class are given the identical amount of time to learn the identical material and receive the identical achievement test to measure what they learned. Under these conditions you will discover that some learned faster than others. You can then give A grades to those who learned the fastest (or knew it all before the instruction began) and F grades to those who learned the slowest (or haven't yet mastered the prerequisite skills). At best, the typical norm-referenced system tells you how fast or how well a student has learned compared to other students. However, if you wish to report *what* a student has learned, the norm-referenced grading system is inadequate.

A more informative grading system to describe students' learning accomplishments is the criterion-referenced system. Here, grades are given on the basis of how well each individual student has achieved the instructional goal chosen for him or her. In a criterion-referenced system, an A means that the pupil has completely mastered a specific task. The grade does not permit you to make any inferences about the performance of any other students in the class. My A does not preclude you from getting an A, as it might in the norm-referenced system with its percentage limit on superior grades. All students who master their instructional goals can achieve A grades in the criterion-referenced system. Some may take 2 days to achieve the goal, and others may take 2 months. How long they took to learn the

material is not important, but only that they eventually did learn it to the predetermined criterion of mastery. Students can work at different levels toward differing goals. Thus, criterion-referenced grading fits individualized education well.

It is not necessary for a whole school district to adopt criterion-referenced grading in order for any individual teacher to try it. Indeed, in accordance with the principle of successive approximations, it might be well for you as an individual teacher to begin experimenting in one small part of the curriculum. For example, after a major spelling test, you might have each child identify 50 (10? 75?) spelling words to learn and say, "I'll give an A to every one of you in spelling as soon as you show me you have mastered your own list." Parents can see the precise list of words their children have mastered. Children can feel good about their accomplishments. Cooperation between children can be enhanced because one child's success does not diminish another child's chances.

And if all your students get A grades in everything you teach, you have not lowered your standards. On the contrary, you have achieved the highest standard—arranging conditions so that each and every student demonstrates maximum progress toward all the goals in your class. That's a noble direction in which to go, but don't think you have to achieve such perfection. Give yourself a pat on the back for every additional step you take toward providing individual success experiences for your pupils.

John D. Krumboltz, PhD, is a professor of education and psychology at Stanford University. **Dr. Laurie Duckham-Shoor** is a counseling psychologist in private practice in San Jose, California. This piece was excerpted from their article in *Theory Into Practice,* October 1977, with permission of the College of Education, Ohio State University.

Classroom court

Here's how a classroom court challenged students to be creative, responsible, and fair—and simplified discipline for the teacher.

As the three black-robed judges entered and took their places, the assembled group rose quietly and stood until the bailiff said to be seated. One of the judges asked the defendant to stand. The charges were read, the defendant pleaded not guilty, and the trial began.

A scene on TV? A film on law? No—my fifth-grade classroom in Colorado Springs, Colo., where all the court participants were students. The "tribunal," as we came to call it, had evolved with surprising speed from a discussion on class rules. The students wanted to take responsibility for the rules they made and were searching for a way to do it. We needed a fair method of dispensing justice when the rules were broken: What better than a court of law? This would allow students to take responsibility for their own behavior. And it would give them hands-on experience in the workings of a judicial system as well.

With only a rough idea of what to expect and dozens of questions, we set out to mold our exciting, untested idea into a workable form. We decided that three judges would hear cases and set penalties for offenders. We added a bailiff who used a gavel to keep order, a court clerk who swore in witnesses, a court recorder who kept the books, and a taper who recorded the proceedings. (The taper was eventually declared unnecessary.) Students filled the positions on a rotating basis.

We discussed the importance of treating each other fairly and of not letting friendships and quarrels get in the way of justice. We made plans to visit a local courthouse in session. Finally, we were ready to get started.

Holding court

One day I asked the class to be completely silent for reading time, but I soon had the names of four talkative boys on the board. The three boys currently serving as tribunal judges felt this was a good time for our first gathering. We arranged our tables and chairs and were ready for the proceedings to begin. Three of the boys pleaded not guilty; one shrugged and admitted, "Yeah, I was talking."

A parade of witnesses then consumed much of our afternoon. Many of them, however, simply repeated what had just been said. Loud arguments and contradictions sprang up. Clearly, we needed more order. So, when the judges retired to their "chambers" for a decision, the rest of the class and I discussed setting guidelines to make the tribunal run more smoothly. We began by limiting the number of witnesses to four. Their names would have to be given in written form to one of the judges before the tribunal began.

The judges returned a verdict of guilty for three of the boys. The guilty boys had to miss both recesses the next day. The punishment was accepted, and our first case was closed.

Define, refine, continue

As the year went on, a pattern developed. Each time we had a tribunal, the class and I used the judges' deliberation time to discuss what changes we'd make to improve the process next time. We gained confidence in our ability to reach fair decisions and solve problems. And we depended upon actual experience to reveal what those problems were.

For example, another case involved two girls who, when accused of running and pushing, felt they'd not been given enough warning to warrant a tribunal. By discussing this, we developed a better system for warning people and for determining when the tribunal was needed. Our solution was to keep a book with everyone's name on a separate page. When someone broke a class rule, the offense was written in the book, signed by the person who wrote it, then signed by the accused. Any student who accumulated three offenses had to face the tribunal.

We discussed whether the consequences should be any different when I, as the teacher, reported an offense. The students favored an automatic tribunal; I suggested that my listing, like a student's, count as only one. The class decision held, so I knew to report only those infractions that warranted the time.

In one case, a witness was caught lying for a friend. That led us into a lively discussion of perjury and the need for truth in court. I was pleased by the high moral standards and idealism expressed by the class. A later case raised the issue of having a lawyer call the witnesses. The class decided this was permissible. Our visit to the local courthouse may have inspired this realistic touch.

We also discussed pleading "not guilty" when you really were guilty. The class consensus? If you *had* misbehaved, admit it and give your reasons. If there was nothing to explain, accept the consequences. We discussed punishment as well. The obvious standby was missing recess, but I encouraged the students to consider punishments that fit the crime. Some tribunals were better than others at this. One assigned a litterer to pick up all the trash on the playground. Another made a pusher take the end position in line for a week.

The teacher's role

As teacher, I was an observer and occasionally a witness, but still in charge of the classroom. If a verdict was unacceptable, I had to modify it. To preclude this, I asked the judges to share their decision with me beforehand if they felt I might question it. I'm pleased to say that I didn't once have to use my veto power.

My qualms about parental reaction were put to rest quickly. At a parents' night early in the year, I explained the tribunal and invited comments. Most parents strongly favored our courtroom system. They expressed confidence in the fairness of their children and encouraged activities that fostered sorting facts, making decisions, and seeing something through to its logical conclusion. One parent hoped his child would learn that authority carries with it the responsibility to be fair and just. Another provided black choir robes for the judges.

The verdict

Whenever we adjourned a session of the tribunal, a feeling of goodwill and closeness prevailed in the room. A wrong had been done; but we had faced it and handled it together. The children grew in respect for themselves and for each other. They knew the tribunal functioned through their decisions and involvement—*their input made a difference*.

The year's over now, and the verdict's in. The tribunal has been found *guilty* of assuring that each student had a chance for leadership and decision making; encouraging students to accept responsibility for their own behavior; helping students to develop compassion and respect for one another; decreasing students' complaints against each other (some sounded embarrassingly petty in court); increasing students' knowledge of our judicial system; becoming an excellent, thriving example of what can happen when fifth-graders' creative and pragmatic talents are challenged.

Sandy Wilson, a former elementary teacher in the Air Force Academy District, Colorado Springs, Colo., now lives in Mill Creek, Wash.

7
MAKING THE MOST OF SPECIAL ACTIVITIES

Breaking up the predictable, daily routine is absolutely necessary from time to time to keep some sparkle in classroom life. Special events and special activities give you and your students something extra to talk about and something special to enjoy in anticipation and later to remember. Read on for some planning and organizing techniques that will take the fear out of field trips and put some fun into science fairs. And for everyday fun, try an easy learning game that you and your students are sure to enjoy more than show-and-tell.

Foolproof field trips

Tired of school? Kids driving you up the wall? Need a break from the humdrum routine? Want to have some fun? As a front-line veteran of many years of middle-school classroom duty, I prescribe a heavy dose of field trips, to be administered according to the following directions.

Break into the field-trip business by finding a teacher who is always hauling kids somewhere. Follow him around. If Paul Pathfinder takes 60 kids to the art museum, go along. If he organizes an overnight camping trip for 25 students, invite yourself. If he's touring the state legislature with his history class, tour there. After three or four trips, you'll know whether you have the guts to strike out on your own. If you don't, go back to your classroom and organize some more study units. But if you're strong enough to try, hang in there—great new vistas in education are about to open before you.

Never underestimate the power of a field trip in the great cosmic scheme of things. It can be the most effective part of the whole

I like to take my country bumpkins UP—in a skyscraper, monument, tower, or whatever.

vicious punishment-reward cycle. Chances are that one kid will actually say to you, "I'm gonna quit makin' trouble. I decided you ain't so bad after all—you're gonna take us on a field trip!" And he *will* shape up, at least until after the trip. He's that glad to be out on parole, even for one day. (Yes, I know your classroom is too exciting and vibrant to be compared to a prison, but think of all the unenlightened teachers that a kid has had to put up with.)

To use the method most effectively, then, the field trip should be scheduled for a school day. Saturdays aren't all bad and will attract a decent gathering, but there's nothing like a blah Wednesday for getting away from it all. Mondays aren't entirely safe because kids forget to come to school with their sack lunches or spending money or cameras or other vital field-trip accoutrements. And I don't much care for Fridays (except in the case of super-long or strenuous trips that require a weekend of recuperation) because I'm sneaky enough to want them to write about and/or discuss the trip the very next day—before their brains congeal.

So pick a date. But regardless of your eagerness to reap those pretrip benefits of good behavior, do *not* announce the trip to the kids at this point. First you must manage to get the project administration-approved—in writing. Failure to do this before you've announced the trip can bring a deafening chorus of "But you *promised*!" down on your head.

Somebody in the charmed circle of administrators is in charge of handing out field-trip application forms. Find out who it is and get one. Then pretend you're taking a test in Education 101 and put down all the right answers, in the most nauseating educationese you can muster. Unless your administrators are among the very few who believe in having fun, don't ever admit that the basic purpose of the trip

is pleasure. It may well be, but lie about it. Somewhere on the page you will find a line that says: "State the specific educational objectives to be accomplished during the course of the proposed trip." Now how the hell should you know? You just want the kids to have a good time hiking and roasting hot dogs. But you're beginning to catch on if you write: "Firsthand study of interesting rural environment should result in retaining several excellent specimens for science laboratory projects. Daily nutritional requirements for the four basic food groups will be demonstrated by careful preparation of the lunchtime repast. Meaningful social interaction in a group dynamics situation will also be an important conceptual goal during the outing." Yes, that ought to about cover it; someone is sure to catch a frog and dissect it while the rest of the crew throws Coke cans at the poor soul who forgot the ketchup.

The trip application form is not all fantasy, however. It will force you to plan details carefully so that you can list the exact type of transportation, the cost, and the time schedule. That's all to the good, because if you can't do that, you have no business going on a trip anyway.

Where should you go?

A good rule of thumb is that city kids ought to go to the country and country kids ought to visit the city. Actually, both ought to do both if possible.

I happen to favor good museums, the kind that have something for everyone. I also like to take my country bumpkins *up*—in a skyscraper, monument, tower, or whatever. An astonishing number of them have never used an elevator or escalator, and it's fun to watch them learn how.

I confess a penchant for the state parks that have naturalist tours, wildlife exhibits, or other educational possibilities.

I'm not so great on the great outdoors. But I'm working on it. I have found state parks to be reasonably safe and interesting. I confess a penchant for the ones that have naturalist tours or wildlife exhibits or historical buildings or other redeeming educational possibilities. But that's probably my own weakness; I know it's easier to supervise kids when at least part of the program is structured. I'm not yet ready to face an entire day of exploring trails, climbing cliffs, wading through streams, and crawling around caves. But I'm working on it

because I know all that's important too.

City kids no doubt would enjoy knocking around an honest-to-income-producing farm for a day. My kids live on them, so they could care less about looking at the baby chicks and the tractors. Now a deluxe corn picker might impress them, but only if its cab is air-conditioned and has a CD player.

Make no mistake about it, impressing them is the name of the game. Arranging a worthwhile field trip is too much work for you to settle for a run-of-the-mill experience. You're shooting for something they'll enjoy enough to remember, maybe even into the second generation. When a former student's kid begins bugging you to take him on a field trip because his dad always used to go fun places when he was in your class, then you'll know you must be doing something right. Either that or you're in a terrible rut.

How do you impress them? By taking them to a place that has impressed you. That might sound obvious, but I have seen teachers who were openly bored by the buildings they dragged their classes through. Not surprisingly, the kids were bored too. But if boredom generates more of the same, enthusiasm does likewise. So go someplace that you really enjoy. You won't have to fake it, and your pleasure will be contagious.

How do you know you'll enjoy a certain place? Because you have been there and enjoyed it recently. First try it out on your own or with a small group of friends or family. If some of them happen to be the same age as your students, so much the better. Watch their reactions. Walk the proposed route, timing yourself, and make the necessary adjustments in the proposed schedule. Pick up leaflets along the way, read them, and haul the more interesting ones back to the classroom with you. Talk to guards, rangers, cops, docents, big shots, or whoever can tell you what you need to know. Find out about discounts and rest rooms and eating facilities and parking lots and all manner of other things that you will be smart enough to ask about if you jot down your questions as you go.

If you lead such an uneventful life that you lack ideas of where to go, there are plenty of places to get suggestions. Write the tourist council in your state capital. Hound the nearby chambers of commerce. Ask a librarian for books to point you in the right direction. Watch for newspaper features or ads of likely spots. Above all, get out and explore on your own.

Who should go on the trip?

Almost everybody. If Johnny gives you a lot of trouble in the classroom, you may be tempted to leave him home. Don't—unless you want Johnny to give you even more trouble ever after. He will put on a big bluffing sour-grapes act about how he didn't want to go anyway, but he will be hurt to the quick. Kids do not like to be singled out as unfit for human companionship. Neither would you. So be an old softie for once—take him along. He may surprise you if you give him a chance. Teachers learn on field trips too, and one of the first things they learn is that kids don't act the same outside a classroom as they do inside. The quiet, well-behaved scholars may be real hell-raisers outside. And vice versa, fortunately. It usually balances out.

How many parents should you invite on the trip? The answer depends on your experience and degree of control, on the nature of the outing, and on how rowdy you think the kids will be. I've known a few Superteacher types who could handle 50 or 60 kids by themselves, but I sure don't recommend that for beginners. An absolute minimum number of adults, I would say, is three: one to lead the caravan, one to mingle with the middle, and one to bring up the rear. Or, one to sit in the front of the bus and make sure the driver knows where he's going, one for the middle, and one in the back, where all the action would otherwise be.

You may want to take many more than three adults. I have been on trips where the ratio of adults to students was 1 to 35, and on others where it was 1 to 4. I think it's best to err in the latter direction. If your students are too big to be treated like babies, yet not quite old enough to be turned loose, just do the best you can. Use your discretion, but do have some help along in case you need it.

OK, so you need some parents. Which ones? Discretion is the key again, combined with plain dumb luck. If you have a student who already depends on his mommy to do everything but breathe for him, that's one mommy you don't invite. Give the kid a break and let him try his own wings for once. You may be tempted to include only the parents of the most popular and best adjusted students; they are most likely to be available and cooperative. But don't fall into this trap. In the first place, their kids may not want a family chaperone tagging along. In the second place, this is a good chance for you to get acquainted with the parents of some of your less exemplary students. Use a mixed bag of parents.

And don't overlook other sources of help. If you have a teacher's aide or student teacher that can be sprung loose to join you, you're in luck. They are doubly valuable because they know the kids' names and are experienced yellers—though only when absolutely necessary, of course. You may be lucky enough to have a principal who enjoys field trips too. That's beautiful. Take him along. If you really get in a mess, he might be able to get you out of it. At the very least, he would make a good scapegoat.

When should you go on a jaunt?

When you're bored to death with school and just have to get out, that's the time to go. And on a Tuesday, Wednesday, or Thursday, as I've already suggested. But a few other elements should be taken into consideration too. Such as the elements themselves. If you live in an area where blizzards or floods are common, you'd be a fool to plan a field trip during the vulnerable season. Even if you won administration approval and even if the buses pulled out on time, you'd be a nervous wreck scanning the sky all day and wondering whether you'd make it back. And there's a definite possibility that you could end up snowbound with 60 kids on a 60-passenger bus with no food (other than bubble gum) and a dwindling fuel supply. So think on that, and plan your trip for the season of fair skies—when everyone else does, when buses and tours are harder to schedule, and when you have a better chance of bringing 'em back alive.

When it comes to picking a date, careful planning far in advance pays off. Far in advance means 6 months or so. Obviously, this isn't necessary if all you're going to do is walk them down the street to the post office for a quick look at the mailbags. But if you want to "do" one of the more popular museums and do it right, 6 months isn't a bit too early to make arrangements.

Don't get so carried away with your planning that every minute is scheduled. If flexibility is important in the classroom, it is even more important in the classroom-on-the-road. You may come across an impromptu band concert in the park or a gorgeous waterfall that you missed on your dry run earlier. It would be a shame to be so tightly locked into a timetable that you couldn't spend a few minutes enjoying whatever unexpected treats come your way.

And don't forget that your charges need to be watered and drained once in a while. Teachers are reportedly human, but sometimes they don't listen to the messages their bodies send—so schedule potty breaks.

✓ How will you get there?

Probably by foot or by bus. Maybe by subway.

If you live in an area where blizzards or floods are common, you'd be a fool to plan a field trip during the vulnerable season.

But not in private cars—on that path lie too many legal hazards.

If you decide to go by foot, make sure you are in good condition. Someone in the athletic department can probably draw up a training program for you. Take it seriously, and stick to it for as many months as you can.

If you choose the subway or city bus, double-check the schedule and route. If possible, ride several days running at the appointed hour, and note how crowded and how late you can realistically expect to be. Adjust your schedule of events accordingly. Also buy tokens ahead of time or warn your students about the importance of having correct change.

Two other kinds of buses warrant your consideration: charter buses and school buses. The former have a big advantage in comfort, but they often are outrageously expensive. If you are prepared to get all wrapped up in money-making projects, go ahead and charter one. Otherwise, consider a bus owned by the school district or by a driver under contract to the district. The cost will range from nothing to moderate-reasonable. If you take lots of trips, you'll soon discover one driver you would trust to take you anywhere. Request him every time, and treat him with respect. He could be the best thing you have going for you.

After computing the transportation cost and collecting for it, check and recheck any admission fees involved in the day's activities. Collect fees in advance to save some weary ticket seller the trouble of dealing with 50 quarter-clutching fists.

Also check and recheck the route, the reservations, and the eating arrangements. If you're going to mess with sack lunches, figure out where to eat them and what to wash them down with. If you're going to a restaurant, a cafeteria, or even a quick hamburger joint, be sure to call and warn the manager. The very least he will want to do is arrange a special room for your group. He might even want to take the day off and leave his assistant manager to cope. Don't, don't, don't ever walk into an eating establishment with a bunch of kids in tow without having called first. And do try to arrive close to the time you're expected.

Making the announcement, getting the permission

Now that you have all the information and the trip is administration-approved, you are at last ready to announce the trip to the class. One way to do this is to hand out notes for them to take home to their mommies and daddies. You'll want to include, as succinctly as possible, all the information about the trip: where you're going and what you'll see, when you're leaving, when you're getting back, what the students need to bring along, what the costs will be for transportation and admission fees, when that money should be sent to school, and a permission slip. The permission slip can be as simple as it needs to be or as legalistic as your school requires. The legalistic permission slip almost certainly wouldn't hold up in court, but most parents are willing to sign a document

like this if necessary. You should, of course, check with the Powers That Be about the acceptable form before you type a stencil for the homebound notes. And while you're at it, run off some extras. Some of your students will lose their notes on the way home, or maybe even on the way out of the classroom.

A surprising number of them, however, will manage to hand the note to a parent, get it signed, collect the required money, and be waiting to hand it over as soon as you reach school the next morning. They may be lurking in the parking lot, at the teachers' entrance to the building, near your mailbox, or at your door. They will beg you to take the money and permission slips out of their hands before they lose them. Don't fall for it. They should hang onto the stuff until the designated turning-in time and place. That's probably going to be during the first few minutes of class. There are all kinds of advantages to this system. You can have them come to the desk one at a time or in some other way that keeps the notes and money piles organized as you take them in. That way you'll never have to search through your coat pockets or briefcase or purse or lunchbag for the note that Sandi says she turned in but you don't remember.

Suppose you get all the notes in but one. And that one kid says his mom won't let him go. Chances are that the family (1) doesn't have the money, or (2) wants to punish the kid for some horrible crime he committed at home, or (3) just plain doesn't trust you to return their precious darling intact. In the event of (1), you may well be able to work out some arrangement whereby you float the kid a loan or let him wash your car or simply inform him that an anonymous donor (guess who?) has offered to award a field-trip scholarship and he's the lucky winner. In the more troubling event of situation (2) or (3), you can try talking

And don't forget that your charges need to be watered and drained once in a while.

to the parents, but you probably won't get anywhere. Tell them about the great educational value of the trip, tell them you'll personally watch their kid, or tell them they should think up some other punishment. But don't count on changing their minds. And beware of stowaways. No permission slip, no trip.

By this time the kids will be bugging you to know exactly what to expect on the Big Day, which is now beginning to assume the proportions of Christmas/Birthday/Fourth of July to some of them. You might as well set aside a generous hunk of class time to go through it all with them. Tell them again where they are going, what they will see, and what they might learn from what they see, hear, smell, touch, and so on. Tell them again about the lunch details, and warn them *not* to wear new shoes. Be sure they know where and when to meet for departure. Try to answer all their questions, but after a reasonable time, shut them off. You all have other work to do.

Tips for the day

Comes the big day, you round them up and count noses before you go. Take roll call from a list you'll carry with you. Also carry with you any letters of confirmation regarding your tours and any maps you might need. Also a needle and thread, a few safety pins, and a tiny first-aid kit. The permission slips you can leave with the principal's secretary, along with a list of any absentees. That way the secretary will know which parents to start calling if there should be a problem during the trip.

If you have decided to assign adults to predetermined subgroups of students (a regrettable but sometimes necessary system), get them together and start the introductions rolling. Then load the bus and take off. Unless your driver objects, let the kids sing and holler and make all the noise they care to make on the way to wherever you're going. With luck, they may let off enough steam to be somewhat subdued when you arrive at the art museum.

When the bus stops, quiet the kids down long enough to listen while you make a few very brief and very necessary statements. If you've been careful about your preparations, you won't have to say much at this point. So don't. Nobody wants to hear you blab. But do be sure they understand who they're going with and where to meet again. It might not hurt to remind them about the dangers of rattlesnakes or jaywalking or whatever seems appropriate. But that's all. Don't load them down with a bunch of dumb rules. If some rules are necessary, be sure they are understood. And obeyed. Then shut up and let them take off.

From the time you get off the bus, you should be able to—well, not quite relax, but at least enjoy yourself to some extent. You picked a place that you could be enthusiastic about, remember? So go ahead and enthuse. Just remember to count noses once in a while. And follow your timetable fairly closely. You do want to get your students and your bus back at the appointed hour. Otherwise lots of people will be worried and inconvenienced, and you may find it difficult to get permission for your next field trip.

Oh yes, there will be another trip. Always. As soon as your students tire of talking or writing about the first one, they'll start hounding you to arrange the next one. And if everything (or even almost everything) goes smoothly the first time, you'll be ready to go again. Just as soon as your blistered feet heal and the ringing in your ears goes away.

Dorothy Rathbun was a free-lance writer and teacher at original publication of this article.

A PLANNING TECHNIQUE THAT WORKS

If you've ever had nightmares about a field trip date arriving before you've had time to make adequate arrangements, you may want to experiment with the backdating technique. Backdating begins with the date of the trip—say, a trip to an apple orchard on October 29—then goes backward to include all the steps in the arrangements leading up to the event. You might also want to add follow-up activities, such as thank-you letters.

Make a list of the steps in chronological order, and estimate how far in advance each step needs to be taken. For example:

Initial contact with orchard: 6 weeks
Transportation arrangements: 5 weeks
Parental permission: 10 days
Reminders to parents: 5 days
Finalize arrangements: 4 days
The lead time will be governed by many factors, of course, including the kind of place you're going and where it's located.

Your own experience with field tripping will be most important in making decisions.

When the list is complete with days-in-advance designations for each step, transfer the information to a calendar, making adjustments for holidays, test times, and other "prior claim" dates.

Once the backdating has been worked out for one event, your chronological list and calendar can serve as resources for future trips. Of course, even the best-laid backdated plans can be guides only, since many critical factors resist scheduling. However, a calendar that reminds you—in the chaos of September—that your apple orchard trip is just 45 days away may help you avoid those uncomfortable, pressed-for-time anxieties later on.

FIELD TRIP GUIDEBOOK

What do you remember about last year's field trip to the harbor or to the post office? How much do you think the children remember? A field trip can be the highlight of the school year, and yet important details can be lost. By preparing a special guidebook in advance of the big trip (and making a class-size quantity of copies), you can assure your students of a truly memorable excursion.

You might want to begin preparation for the guidebook this summer, while there's time to send for descriptive material and to do either on-site or at-home research about the to-be-visited location. Possible items to incorporate into a field trip guidebook include:

—a capsule background of the destination;

—comments and questions to guide observation, preferably in as-you'll-see-it order;

—reminders of field trip safety and courtesy measures;

—space for students to write trip-related questions to be taken up later in class;

—suggestions for follow-up projects and research;

—space for students to summarize and comment on their field trip experience.

The guidebook's cover design can be a general-purpose one—to serve for several field trips—with space for students to write their names, the field trip destination and date, and the name of their partner, teacher, and school.

This year, make that harbor excursion one for the books.

Take an armchair field trip

How would you like to have a member of the United States House of Representatives drop into your classroom to discuss legislation pending in Congress? Wouldn't it be great if your students could interview the author of the book you are reading in class now? You would surely enjoy having experts from all over the country come in to share their knowledge and ideas with your students.

Impossible? Too expensive? That's what we used to think. Yet in the last few years, our classrooms have been favored with visits from writers, religious leaders, numerous state and local officials, university professors, and even the St. Louis Blues hockey team.

The expense in each case has been minimal—basically, the cost of a phone call. By using a speakerphone, we've introduced students to resource people from all over the nation—and indeed could bring them from anywhere in the world.

The speakerphone, available from electronic stores as well as telephone companies, is surprisingly compact. Many are identical to regular telephones except for a built-in speaker which amplifies the caller's voice and a built-in microphone which permits anyone in the room to talk without using the handset.

One of our most memorable visitors was the Reverend Jesse Jackson. We placed the conference call on the occasion of Martin Luther King, Jr.'s birthday, and the Reverend Jackson spoke for 15 minutes of the work of Dr. King. After the call, we made additional copies of the tape for other schools in our system.

Nearby experts

Few of our calls are made to national celebrities. Most are made to persons in our city or the surrounding area. We frequently call state and local officials and instructors and professors from nearby colleges and universities. The chance to speak with and question these people has given our students a broader view of the world outside the classroom.

Teachers may also find the speakerphone a rich resource for purposes beyond classroom instruction. For example, when we were sponsoring a teaching workshop for local volunteers, we wanted to demonstrate our strong support of the program, but we didn't have enough money to bring in a well-known keynote speaker. The problem was solved by arranging for the Illinois State Superintendent of Education to meet the group by telephone. The call lasted 45 minutes—about the time of an ordinary address—and the interview format let participants ask about other volunteer programs in the state as well as explore the problems connected with volunteerism. The call was economical in terms of time and money. The superintendent did not have to spend time preparing a speech, traveling to and from Quincy, or sitting through any other speeches. Our district incurred no hotel, meal, or transportation expenses. The cost of the phone call: about $10.

Starting out right

The cost of a speakerphone is about the same as any good quality telephone. Less expensive units, designed for small groups, are appropriate for occasional classroom use. For districts utilizing a speakerphone often, however, it would be wise to invest in a higher quality model. No matter what model you choose,

make sure you try it out in the classroom before you buy. The volume and audio quality may be fine in the store but unsatisfactory in the classroom.

Once the unit is purchased, teachers can help ensure its successful use by following these suggestions:

Make arrangements for the call well in advance. We usually write a letter to the resource person 4 to 6 weeks prior to the call, suggesting alternative dates and times. About a week before the call, we send a postcard reminding the person of the date and time agreed upon.

Let the resource person know what your class is expecting. Be sure to clarify the following points: what subjects will be covered; what type of format will be used; whether there should be an opening statement, and if so, on what topic. We've found that a short opening statement followed by questions and answers usually works best.

Plan the call with your students. We have our students submit questions ahead of time and then pick the most relevant for the interview. The questions must deal with the resource person's area of expertise. A United States senator, for example, would not ordinarily be asked questions about local politics, sports, or music. After the resource person's opening statement, student questioners line up at the phone, ready to ask their questions. This helps save time and money, and minimizes pauses and silences.

Agree on a time limit and stick to it. In the initial contact, we always set a time limit, usually 30 minutes. During an exceptionally interesting interview, it is tempting to go beyond the half-hour limit. Avoid the temptation; it isn't fair to the resource person. If, on the other hand, it is the resource person who asks to continue the conversation, and if your budget can afford it, by all means go ahead.

Check the cost of the call ahead of time. You probably will need to get permission from your principal or director to make a long-distance call. This is easier to do if you know exactly what the rates are. Remember that rates are lower for calls dialed directly.

Consider speaking with more than one resource person during the same call. We learned about this possibility by accident. On one occasion, a congressman had to leave a telephone interview for an important committee vote. He handed the phone to another well-known congressman who was in his office at the time. "Here," he said to the man. "This is a United States history class in my district. Tell them about the energy bill you're proposing." If you can arrange an interview with two or more legislators who differ in basic philosophy or on specific issues, your class can benefit doubly.

Be sure the resource person understands that the call is for educational purposes and that there will be no pay. While we have never had anyone refuse to participate because there was no pay involved, it is better to have this understanding before the call rather than after it.

Ask permission to tape the call. Taped interviews can be kept for playback in other classes and for future reference. You should make it clear, however, that the tape will only be used in local schools, and will not otherwise be reproduced and distributed.

Consider visuals. The "telelecture" may be made that much more meaningful by the inclusion of relevant visuals—slides, photographs, pictures from books or magazines. Check with the resource person beforehand for suggestions.

Follow up with a thank-you letter. Everyone appreciates a note of gratitude. Resource people may especially enjoy personally written letters from the students themselves.

Don't be afraid to think small. This may seem strange advice, but we've found that the portable conference telephone is so versatile and has so much potential that teachers tend to think too big: "Let's get Jerry Lewis to talk about comedy." "How about calling the Secretary of State about the Middle East situation?" Resource people of super magnitude are usually hard to get and far away, but experts of only slightly less renown may be available at a nearby university. Again, be sure you don't overlook the experts in your own community. A judge, for example, might not be able to visit your classes, but could find time for a short telephone call. Resource people who might be self-conscious appearing in person before a group of students may find a phone visit far less intimidating.

In spite of all the potential uses and benefits of the speakerphone, it is still not widely used in schools. Asked why, a local telephone company representative said, "I don't know. Too expensive, I guess."

Too expensive? The speakerphone gives our school the capability of traveling anywhere in the world. Experts from every conceivable field can be brought into our classrooms. Our students can meet and interview legislators and other newsmakers. We think it's one of the most reasonably priced resources we have.

Don Blattner is the director of media for the Quincy School District in Quincy, Ill.

Put some snap into your science fair

Last spring, I visited a science fair sponsored by one of the local elementary schools. Two things immediately caught my attention.

First was the lack of originality. Most of the projects were just like ones I've seen at other science fairs—a half-dozen volcanoes, several models of the solar system, and lots of experiments with plants. Second, and more appalling, was the lack of enthusiasm. I'd expected the fair to be packed with projects and people. I saw neither. This school had over 500 students, yet fewer than 60 projects were on display. A scattering of people shuffled about, raising hardly more than a murmur.

If that description sounds familiar, or if you'd just like to put more life into your science fair, try these suggestions.

Stir up enthusiasm ahead of time

Have an "everyone wins" science fair. This means every child who enters a project that meets predetermined minimum standards is guaranteed a ribbon. These ribbons should be the same size and quality as the first-place ribbons; the larger ribbons should be the grand-prize awards that single out an excellent project at each grade level.

Before you announce your "everyone wins" science fair, start drumming up attention. Set up a display someplace where students are sure to see it, maybe in a hallway or the cafeteria. Include lots of pictures of previous science fair projects and show the awards that can be won. Be sure to post the rules and important dates. Ask your school librarian to set up a science center with reference materials as well as science books and filmstrips.

Next, have a special pep rally to get students excited about the science fair. Don't go over

rules (this can be done later in the classroom). Instead, show a film or have a guest speaker—perhaps someone from an environmental group, a utility company, or a government agency, like NASA. End the rally by telling your students about the ribbons they'll receive if they enter.

Follow the rally with a weekly science fair newsletter. Keep it brief, but include announcements, tips for better projects, and a question-and-answer section.

Give overworked off projects a year

If you're tired of seeing the same old projects, simply exclude them ahead of time. Announce, "This year we will not accept any solar systems (or volcanoes, or whatever's been overworked) for science fair projects."

Expect some groans. These projects are popular with students because they're interesting and easy to build. Capitalize on that popularity by featuring these topics in classroom lessons. Encourage your students to come up with novel approaches to the worn-out project and original ways to display it.

One teacher, tired of seeing volcanoes, had each of her students build a volcano for a classroom science fair, then awarded ribbons for the most original display. Not only did she stop her students from entering an overworked project in the schoolwide fair, but she also used their interest in volcanoes to teach them how to present a fresh science fair project. So if you exclude certain projects from the science fair, be sure you include them in your classroom instruction.

Issue a challenge

A challenge gets your students doing more experimentation and problem solving. Hold these challenges several weeks before the science fair. Take plenty of pictures (videotape if possible) and display them along with the students' challenge projects as a special exhibit at the science fair.

Here are some challenges you can choose from:

Tower Challenge. Build a tower 6 inches high that will support more weight than any other student-built tower. Limit construction materials to wood (toothpicks, popsicle sticks, or tongue depressors), paper, tape, and glue. The lightest structure that holds the most weight is the winner. Remember to weigh each structure *before* testing its strength.

Flight Challenge. Design a hand-powered airplane that will fly 30 feet. The heaviest plane to travel the required distance wins.

Egg Drop Challenge. Construct a protective device that will prevent a raw egg from breaking when it's dropped from a height of 10 feet and hits the ground. In case of a tie, the lightest container is the winner.

Insulation Challenge. Build a container that will prevent an ice cube from melting. Make ice cubes from equal amounts of water, seal each ice cube in a plastic bag, and store it in a freezer. When you're ready to begin, have your students put one bag into their containers. Set the containers aside at room temperature for an hour; then remove the bags and measure the amount of water in them. The winner is the bag with the least amount of water.

America's Cup Challenge. Design a sailboat that will travel across a linoleum or hardwood floor when placed in front of a room fan. The boat that travels the farthest wins—wheels are not allowed.

Try new categories

Most science fairs have three categories: physical science, life science, and earth science. By adding one or two new categories, you can direct your students to areas of science they may have otherwise overlooked. Here are some categories you can try:

Science in History. Have your students re-create famous experiments, discoveries, or de- velopments in science. In this category, your students would enter projects like the Archimedes screw, the development of communication, or the history of antibiotics.

Science Today. Projects in this category examine recent discoveries in medicine, space, electronics, and other scientific fields. Students design their projects to clearly and accurately explain these discoveries. Sample titles include "What is a Microchip?," "Dinosaur Renaissance," and "Lasers."

Topical. Unlike the Science Today category, the Topical category addresses popular issues and topics of the day. If you listen to what people are talking about, to what's on television and in the newspapers, you can usually find a great topical category. During the energy crisis, one school had a category for energy-related projects. Special ribbons were given to the best projects in the energy category. Among the entries were solar heating systems, wind generators, and energy conservation plans.

Lately, microcomputers have become popular. For projects in this category, students could build calculators, design programs, invent a video game, experiment with binary numbers, or compare the software of different companies.

Consumer Product Testing. Students can test common household products for safety, effectiveness, and value. They can test one product or compare different brands. Entries in this category might have names like "Hidden Costs of Paper Towels," "Light Bulbs: A Comparison of Brands," or "What Kind of Battery Lasts the Longest."

Look for other special categories that are peculiar to your school or region. By adding one or two new categories, you create interest and expand the number of project ideas available to your students.

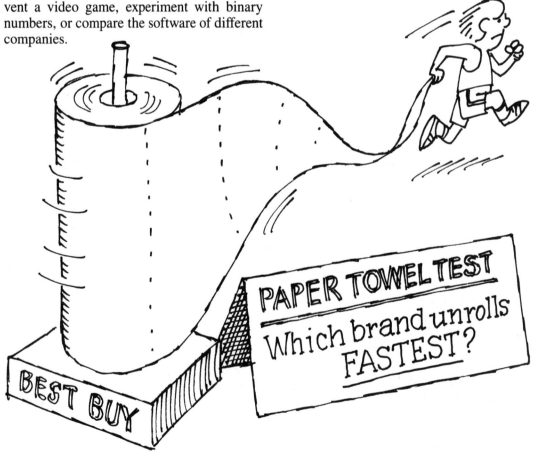

Add variety to the judging

Judges have to follow the guidelines you give them, so take a look at your judging criteria. If projects lack creativity, maybe it's because creativity is worth only 25 points out of a possible 100. The same can be true for scientific thought. Boost the points assigned to a criterion, and you'll boost enthusiasm for that criterion.

Also, try different judging teams in addition to your regular judges. Let students, teachers, and parents form teams and give out special awards: a Student Award, a Teacher Award, a Parent Award. By including more people as judges, you're adding interest to your science fair.

Involve the community

Invite science-related clubs and organizations to participate. Astronomy clubs may set up telescopes on the playground for public viewing; user groups and computer merchants may display their skills and products. Encourage people to show their private collections of rocks and minerals, flowers, insects, and butterflies. Involving the community doesn't overshadow the work of your students; instead, it adds an exciting dimension by showing students that science interests extend to the adult world.

Have an appreciation day

After the science fair is over, give your students a special day of appreciation for all their work. Make the day festive—not just to reward students for this year's work, but also to motivate them for next year's.

Start off with an awards assembly. The principal should call each participant forward, shake his or her hand, and present the award

along with congratulations. The principal should introduce everyone who helped with the science fair, thank them, and give them special awards. If one person was in charge of the whole science fair, the principal should give him or her an enormous ribbon to wear for the day. Ask your PTA or Parent Club to rent a special movie for the entire school to see and to provide free ice cream for each student who entered a project.

These suggestions can inject new life into your school science fair. But don't wait until your fair gets dull and predictable before you try them. Remember: A milliliter of prevention is worth a liter of cure.

Myron Flindt teaches at Ponderosa Elementary School, Paradise, Calif.

Forget Show-and-Tell

The Paper Bag Guessing Game is my solution to Show-and-Tell.

I banned Show-and-Tell from my primary classroom 17 years ago. I'd come to think of it as "Bring-and-Brag." My growing discomfort with the custom reached its limit when Anna, a delightfully exuberant if over-privileged youngster, wheeled in a new doll carriage overflowing with a bounty of birthday presents from her doting grandparents. That was it for Show-and-Tell.

Five years ago, finally, the Paper Bag Guessing Game presented itself as a suitable alternative. A fellow teacher was using the game as an exercise in logic for fifth graders. I borrowed it intact as a way for first and second graders to show something without showing off.

The Paper Bag Guessing Game is a simple extension of the familiar Twenty Questions. The child whose turn it is brings in *one* secret item—owned, borrowed, found—that can be put into a paper bag. The child chooses a classmate to be the "counter-downer," who sits beside the secret-owner and keeps track of how many questions are asked and how many the class has left. Members of the class try to guess what the item is before the 20 questions—yes or no answers only—are used up. (Sometimes a hint or a review of what has already been found out is asked for and given.)

The challenge of the game tends to overrule vanity. Amy, whose doctor father had given her every material possession that a seven-year-old could want, chose one of the hardest-to-guess secret objects—a chunk of broken sidewalk she found on the way to school.

Deeper meanings?

The Paper Bag Guessing Game might pass simply as another good little teacher trick to liven up the day. Yet I have no doubt that the game is as valuable as it is entertaining. First of all, there is the matter of the questions. What *is* a question anyway? First and second graders do not automatically understand. They must work to recognize whether the words they are using do indeed form a question. They struggle to raise the pitch of their voices in order to fit the criteria of a question.

And then, what makes a *good* question? I try to tell the children that every question in the game theoretically should reduce the possibilities by half. This is a rule from the folk knowledge of Twenty Questions (as well as a

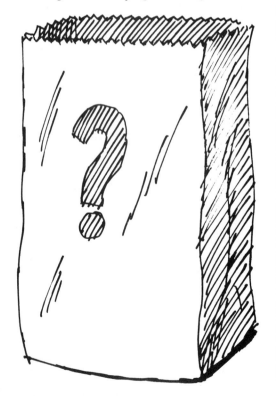

strategy of computer-based problem solving). But it is difficult, so I soften the instruction to: "Try to make each question eliminate more than one possibility. For instance, ask, 'Can you play with it?' or 'Is it something to read?' before asking, 'Is it your laser gun?' or 'Is it *Farmer Boy*?'"

Those who have learned this strategy of question asking can become quite impatient with those who have not. They become frustrated when no amount of explaining on their part seems to clarify for their classmates the point of the open-ended question. They forget their own earlier confusion about this concept.

There is even less patience shown the asker of the "wasted" question. "You wasted a question!" is about as serious an accusation as can be made during the game. Yet who is to judge what is "wasted"? When Sam asked, "Is it little?" followed by Tommy asking, "Is it small?" Sam was indignant that Tommy had "wasted" a question. Tommy was equally indignant that Sam did not understand his gesture indicating that "small" was less than half an inch, while "little" was ever so much bigger.

I tend to stay out of the assessing and correcting of questions, preferring to listen to the children's own problem-solving strategies. I will intervene only after each child who wants to has had a say, and only when I feel that the children need my assurance that the game is proceeding fairly.

New perspectives

There is something in this game for me, too. First, there is the shifting of roles. I become a member of the class, able to pay attention, daydream, enjoy the process of the classroom from the sidelines.

I truly appreciate what a good job the secret-owner and the counter-downer, in charge of this meeting, are doing to keep the game moving and the class organized. I am amused and flattered to hear them echo my own typical responses, as when the secret-owner acknowledges a child with, "That's a very good question" or prods, "Try asking that another way. Take your time. I can wait." I begin to feel good about what I've modeled/taught as students demonstrate what they have learned.

I also have the opportunity to refine my own skills. I practice listening. Can I, in fact, remember all the clues, so that when students ask for a review at various points during the game, I can summarize the information quickly and sequentially? I practice my own logical thinking, trying to devise questions that, if I'm called upon, will reduce the possibilities by half.

Above all, I use the time to observe and learn from each child's behavior. I notice interests, responses, body language, ways of getting attention. At the same time, students have a chance to see me in a different role, from another perspective. It helps us become more visible to one another as human beings.

The game seems in such ways to move us toward an understanding of logic *and* an understanding of human styles and intentions. When the secret item is guessed, it is as much through the interweaving of information gained from questions asked as through what is known about those things the secret-owner values. Certainly the game provides for students and teacher alike the opportunity to use the powers of logic, reason, intuition, and understanding. And yet, without any of these justifications, I know that the time is valuable, a time of real learning integration.

Molly Watt was a teacher and educational consultant at original publication of this article.

Index

A

Aerial photo of school neighborhood, as welcoming activity, 22

Animal Name game, 75

Anxiety, first-day, helping student to overcome, 30-31

B

Backsliding by student, after behavior change, 142-143

Back-to-school quiz, as welcoming activity, 22, 26

Barnyard game, 77-78

Beanbag relay, 89

Before-school activities, 97

Behavior

changing, 142-143, 150-155

developing rules for, 132-135, 137-139

disruptive, control of, 144-149

observation of, through Five Squares game, 64-74

positive attitude toward, 143

rewarding improvement in, 150-155

successive approximation, effect of, on, 152-155

of teacher, evaluation of, 13

using consequences to improve, 132-135

Behavioral contracting, 150-151

Big Siblings Club, as get-acquainted activity, 45

Birds, as class pets, 121-122

Birthday wheel, as opening activity, 30

B Is for Bonnie game, 79

Book, new, correct way to open, 111

Bulletin board

displays, basics of, 116

ideas for, 14

of questions, as welcoming activity, 25

C

Calendar, circular, 14-16

Catch the Tail tag, 87

Chalkboard maintenance, 111

Choo-Choo tag, 87

Classified ad, as welcoming activity, 20

Class interview, as get-acquainted activity, 45

Class meetings, 138, 139

Class profile, graph of, as opening activity, 27-28

Classroom court, 156-157

Classroom management

evaluation of, 13

groups-of-four scheme for, 54-63

prescriptions for, 5

Closet, storage units for, 106

Collection(s)

approaches to, 124-125

class example of, 128

displaying, 127-128

making sense of, 126-127

variety in, 128-129

Collective collections, 125

Community leaders, as back-to-school keynoters, 20

Consensus, achieving, on rules/consequences, 135-136

Consequences of rule breaking, development of

by students for teacher, 133-135

by students for themselves, 135

by teacher for students, 133

Consequences vs. punishments, for rule breaking, 132

Consistency, need for, in implementing consequences, 138, 141

Cooperative problem solving, 58-63

Creative expression, as get-acquainted activity, 44

Criterion-referenced grading system, 155

D

Dial-a-Day booklets, 16-17

Discipline, method of

criteria for, 141-143

positive attitude as asset to, 143

reality therapy, 134, 137-140

three-dimensional, 132-136

Discipline problems, dealing with, 144-149

Disruptive behavior, controlling, 144-149

Duck-Duck-Goose tag, 86